the
Ultimate
Mailbox
Book

08. 01 2006 New Jersey

the Ultimate Mailbox Book

30
DELIGHTFUL PROJECTS
TO BUILD, PAINT, STENCIL,
MOSAIC & OTHERWISE DECORATE

Danielle Truscott
Catharine Sutherland

LARK BOOKS

A DIVISION OF STERLING PUBLISHING CO., INC.
NEW YORK

CHRIS BRYANT
Book design and production

EVAN BRACKEN
Photography

J. P. DELANOYE
Illustrations

MEGAN KIRBY
Production assistance

**IF YOU HAVE QUESTIONS OR
COMMENTS ABOUT THIS BOOK,
PLEASE CONTACT:**

*Lark Books
50 College Street
Asheville, NC 28801
828.253.0467*

Library of Congress Cataloging-in-Publication Data

Dawson, D.T., 1965–
    The ultimate mailbox book : 30 distinctive & delightful projects
to build, paint, stencil, mosaic, decoupage, & otherwise decorate /
by D.T. Dawson & Catharine Sutherland.—1st ed.
        p.   cm.
     ISBN 1-57990-153-0 (hardcover)
        1. Handicraft.   2. Decoration and ornament.   3. Mailboxes
    I. Sutherland, Catherine.   II. Title
     TX157.D382   1999
     745.5—dc21   99-046246
                                                       CIP

10 9 8 7 6 5 4 3 2 1

First Edition

Published by Lark Books,
a division of Sterling Publishing Co., Inc.
387 Park Avenue South
New York, N.Y. 10016

© 2000 by Lark Books

Distributed in Canada by Sterling Publishing,
c/o Canadian Manda Group, One Atlantic Ave., Suite 105
Toronto, Ontario, Canada M6K 3E7

Distributed in Australia by Capricorn Link (Australia)
Pty Ltd., P.O. Box 6651, Baulkham Hills, Business Centre, NSW 2153, Australia

Printed in Hong Kong by H&Y Printing Ltd.

ISBN 1-57990-162-X

Contents

Introduction

THERE'S nothing quite like opening your mailbox to find that a hoped-for correspondence from a friend, family member, or other loved one has arrived. In fact, the experience of checking the mail holds priceless emotional treasures: the heady feeling of anticipation that surfaces as you feel the promising weight of a letter in your had; the delicious sense of contents almost yours as you open a stamp-laden box; and the joy of savoring feelings and thoughts expressed by someone near and dear. And, of course, there's always the rush of sheer delight upon pulling the packing out of a box to discover a wonderful gift lying in wait!

Of course, not everything received in the mail is so delightful—there's nothing like an astronomical bill or a pile of junk mail to put a little dent in your day. Still, checking the mail—even if the box holds nothing more than an echo—is a ritual we perform every day, as much a routine as getting dressed in the morning or turning off the lights when we go to sleep at night. So why not make the experience special every day by turning your mailbox into an object of beauty, whimsy, or interest?

This book will help you do just that, and provide you with lots of hours of crafting fun at the same time. The 30 projects you'll find on the following pages include a variety of techniques, from painting to stencilling, collage to woodburning, woodworking to metalworking, decoupage to mosaics, all kinds of innovative decorat-ing approaches, and more. Some of the projects are simple, some are sophisticated—the range of styles provides for just about every taste. Whether the look you're after is toned-down and dignified, fresh and contemporary, bright and whimsical, rustic, hip, plain old pretty, or truly unique, you'll be sure to find a mailbox to make that will suit your needs.

Once you've found the one you want, it's time to get under way! A couple of quick trips to the craft-supply or home-improvement store, and you're all ready to start creating a sturdy, super-looking mailbox that will give you pleasure for years to come.

CHAPTER

1

Getting Started

The 30 projects in this book offer a broad variety of ways to decorate and embellish purchased ready-made mailboxes, and loads of easy techniques for building unique, decorative mailboxes from wood (along with one metalworking project for folks who like to do or want to try a bit of simple welding).

You won't need to go far afield to gather the materials and tools required to make the projects you'll find on the following pages. Whether you opt to construct a one-of-a-kind box from scratch or transform a plain store-bought mailbox into a neighborhood conversation piece, a trip to your local craft supply store or home improvement center and/or lumberyard will turn up all of the stuff necessary to make your own great mailbox.

Each project description includes its own detailed list of required materials and tools. But before you set off to hunt and gather any items you don't already have around the house, here's the basic lowdown on what you'll be looking for in the way of tools and materials and how to use them (generally, and in accordance with governmental regulations). You'll also find other helpful information on where and how to install your mailbox once it's completed.

Materials

Theoretically, a mailbox can be made of just about any material imaginable, as long as it is sturdy, stable, conforms to postal service standards, and will withstand rain, shine, wind, snow, and other tests with which the forces of nature may challenge it. (It's not a bad idea to bear in mind and to prepare for the fact that the forces of nature have been known to include a carload of 16-year-olds playing percussion on unsuspecting mailboxes with a baseball bat!) The tried and true materials are not so without due cause, though. So while a mailbox made from some unorthodox, interesting material may look great, it's best to go with a known quantity to ensure that your mail stays clean and dry, and the post office doesn't come calling with a reprimand.

Manufactured Mailboxes

Ready-made, standard-sized mailboxes are available in both post- and wall-mount styles in metal, wood, and plastic. The size of standard-size curbside post-mount mailboxes varies slightly. In some of the woodworking projects in this book, you'll build a structure to fit over or around a manufactured mailbox. This means you need to compare the size of your mailbox with the project dimensions before beginning, and adjust the dimensions to fit your mailbox, if necessary. Wall-mount versions may be square or rectangular (oriented horizontally or vertically) in a very wide range of sizes.

Since plastic tends not to hold up as long as metal or wood (nor, let's face it, particularly lends itself to gasps of delight at its beauty), none of the projects in this book are made using a plastic box. The standard-sized metal or wooden mailboxes you will need for all decorating and some woodworking projects can be inexpensively purchased at a good hardware store or home improvement store in your area. There are also a number of companies that manufacture specialty and higher-end mailboxes, if you want a fancier overall look or choose to adapt one of our projects' designs or techniques to a mailbox in a different shape or size.

Homemade Mailboxes

Wood

Many different types of wood can be and are used to construct homemade mailboxes, but exterior-grade plywood and pine in standard dimensions are the least expensive and most commonly used.

Plywood, which typically comes in 4- x 8-foot (120 x 240 cm) sheets in thicknesses of 1/16 to 3/4 inches (1.5 mm to 1.9 cm), is fabricated from a combination of hardwood (such as oak, maple, or cherry) and softwood (such as pine, fir, or hemlock). It is made of many thin sheets, or "plies," of wood glued with their grains at right angles to one another to form a single sheet of wood. Because each alternated ply's action counteracts that of the one beside it, plywood's expansion and shrinkage are minimal compared to those of other types of wood. This, along with the fact that plywood is easy to cut and fasten, makes it a great choice for mailbox construction. Plywood comes in a variety of grades determined by the quality of the appearance of the top, or outside, face of the sheet. For mailbox construction, you won't need a top-grade plywood. A medium-grade or even low-grade exterior plywood made with waterproof glue will work just fine.

Pine is a widely available softwood which can be purchased in easy-to-work-with dimension lumber sizes. When buying pine for a mailbox construction project, check to make sure that the boards you pick are not crooked, nor riddled with knots—weak spots, where a limb or branch was sunk in the tree, that look like little whorls. If you are new to purchasing dimension lumber, also be aware that the sizes given are nominal, not actual sizes of the pieces of wood they describe. Refer to the table below when making your purchases.

Softwood Lumber Sizes

NOMINAL	ACTUAL
1 x 2	3/4" x 1 1/2"
1 x 4	3/4" x 3 1/2"
1 x 6	3/4" x 5 1/2"
1 x 8	3/4" x 7 1/4"
1 x 10	3/4" x 9 1/4"
1 x 12	3/4" x 11 1/4"
2 x 2	1 1/2" x 1 1/2"
2 x 4	1 1/2" x 3 1/2"
2 x 6	1 1/2" x 5 1/2"
2 x 8	1 1/2" x 7 1/4"
2 x 10	1 1/2" x 9 1/4"
2 x 12	1 1/2" x 11 1/4"
4 x 4	3 1/2" x 3 1/2"
4 x 6	3 1/2" x 5 1/2"
6 x 6	5 1/2" x 5 1/2"
8 x 8	7 1/2" x 7 1/2"

All of the woodworking projects in the following chapters specify types, amounts of, and cut lists for wood (mostly plywood or pine). If you choose to use another type of wood, pick up a woodworking book or talk with a worker at your local lumberyard to familiarize yourself with its properties before starting to saw and hammer.

Fasteners

Nails

For a few of the woodworking projects, you'll use small common nails to secure parts of the mailbox to one another. Common nails, like most nails, come in a range of lengths from 1 to 6 inches (2.5 to 15 cm), with their diameters increasing slightly with length. A common nail's length is described by its "penny size"—a 1-inch (2.5 cm) common nail is referred to as a "twopenny" or "2d" nail.

Screws

Because screws have greater staying power than nails, many of the woodworking projects in this book use as fasteners screws installed either with a screwdriver or a power drill with screw bit. Screws come in a wide range of diameters in lengths up to 6 inches (15 cm) with flat, round, and oval heads; the materials list accompanying each project will tell you which type of screw will work best for that project's requirements. You'll use small, general-purpose flathead or "wood" screws, countersunk so that their heads lie flush with the wood's surface, for most projects.

Wood glue

Wood glue, also known as "carpenter's glue," is often used in combination with nails or screws to fasten pieces of wood together. Only a few of the projects you'll come across in this book call for using wood glue. But it's not a bad idea to have some at the ready, to help strengthen a tricky point of attachment.

Finishes

Because of the wide spectrum of decorating techniques used in this book, different kinds of paint will work better for different projects, and each project's instructions specify the best paint to use. Acrylic artist's paint, which you can pick up at an art or craft store, is required for many of the metal-mailbox painting projects. For wooden mailboxes that you both build and paint, exterior-grade latex or oil paints are the best bet, though interior paints and acrylic paints can be sprayed with polyurethane or clear varnish to finish and seal them. (Some projects involving painting manufactured metal boxes will require a coat of spray varnish or other sealer, too.) Whenever you are painting a wooden box, it's a good idea to apply a coat of primer before starting the painting process itself.

Tools

Most of the tools you'll need for the decorating projects are simple items you probably already have around the house—scissors or a craft knife, a pencil or marker, masking tape, glue, a ruler or measuring tape. If not, you'll find them in an office supply or craft supply store. (The only less common tool, a woodburner, can also be purchased at a craft supply store.)

Making the woodworking projects in this book means using some basic carpentry tools, but most require nothing more daunting than a hammer and nails, screwdriver and screws, and a hand saw. You'll need some simple power tools—a power drill (and bits) and jigsaw, scroll saw, or band saw—for a few of the more complex mailboxes. If you've never had any experience using these, you may want to practice on a piece of scrap wood first, have a more experienced friend or family member give you tips on or a hand with using them, or refer to a good basic woodworker's manual (your local library will more likely than not turn up several up-to-date, comprehensive options, or head to a home improvement center and pick one up there).

Basic Setup and Safety

Along with the specific tools and materials you'll need to build and/or decorate the mailboxes presented as projects in the following chapters, there are some more general items you'll want to have on hand. Whether you're woodworking, painting, decoupaging, or making a mosaic-covered mailbox, a sturdy, level work surface—whether a worktable or coun-tertop or the floor of your garage—is a must. Keep a canvas or plastic drop cloth or some old newspapers on hand, to spread over and cover areas that might get damaged while you're painting, gluing, or using other substances that can stick to or stain surfaces. Likewise, an old plastic bowl, access to water, and an old rag or two will come in handy for cleaning up small messes or mistakes. Be sure to fol-low all manufacturer's instructions and wear safety gear—safety glasses and gloves—when you are using tools for cutting wood or metal.

Mounting and Installing Your Mailbox

Manufactured posts for mounting mailboxes come in wood, metal, and plastic, in a variety of plain and deco-rative styles, and can be purchased at a good hardware store, a home improvement center, or from one of sev-eral good mail-order mailbox suppliers. All are accompa-nied by detailed instructions for both mounting the box and installing it to make your work a lot easier.

If you're feeling ambitious and want to build your own post, here are some options.

Wooden Posts

For Boxes with Recessed Bottoms

While a 2 x 4 post sharpened at one end will do the job, it won't hold up particularly well to time, the weather, or a vehicular nudge. Better to use a pressure-treated 4 x 4 post sharpened to a point at one end for installation. To attach a standard mailbox with a ¾-inch-deep (1.9 cm) bottomside recess, cut a piece of ¾-inch (1.9 cm) plywood to the dimensions of the recess, center and secure the to-size plywood to the top of the post with a few 1½ inch (3.8 cm) screws, and fit the mailbox over the plywood.

For Boxes with Flat Bottoms

Just as for a box with a recessed bottom, a 4 x 4 post sharpened to a point at one end for installation will work fine as a post for a flat-bottomed box. Though attaching a box with a flat bottom is slightly more complex than doing so for a recessed box, it's still easy and will take little time and effort. Cut a 2 x 4 into two pieces of the same width as the mailbox, and secure these to the front and back of the post and flush with its top edge. Next, cut a piece of ¾-inch (1.9 cm) exterior ply-wood to the dimensions of the bottom of your mailbox, and secure this mounting platform with screws to the positioned 2 x 4 pieces. Attach the mail-box to the mounting platform with screws.

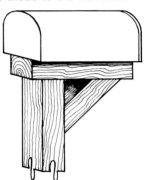

Extra Support for Wood-Post Mounts (Arms and Braces)

If you want to give your mounted mailbox extra support, there are a couple of easy ways to do so. A simple lap-joined arm added to your 4 x 4 post and supported by a wooden or metal brace will provide solid additional strength for your mounted box.

Use another 4 x 4 for the arm, cut to the length you desire. You'll want the arm to extend the length of the mailbox on the side of the post facing the road, to hold the box in place; the arm's exten-sion on the back side of the post should be at least a few inches, though the length is flexible depending on the look you want to achieve. Once it is cut, posi-tion the arm across the post and mark with a pencil lines on both sides of the arm and on the post where the two meet.

With a saw, make a series of close cuts on both 4 x 4s between the lines you've drawn and at about

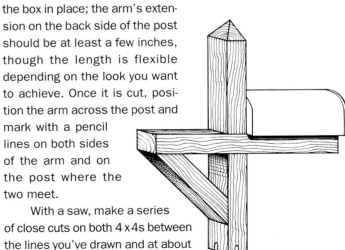

half the depth of the boards. Remove the wood at the cut points with a hammer and chisel to create notches on both boards, then use the notches as a guide to cross-position the post and arm and secure the two with screws.

Once in place, the arm must be braced. The easiest route for bracing is to pick up a metal L-brace, which comes in a range of sizes, at your local hardware store or home improvement center. If you want to build your own wooden brace, it's a snap. Just measure the diagonal between the back edge of the arm and the back of the post, and cut a piece of 4 x 4, angled to 45° on both ends, to these dimensions. Secure it to the arm and post with screws, and you've got a super-sturdy mount for your mailbox!

Metal

While a metal post won't have the more crafted appeal of a wooden post, it's a quick and extremely easy solution to mounting your mailbox. A substantial metal pipe with one threaded end, purchased at a home improvement center, can be fitted with a floor flange at the threaded end. The box can then be fitted with a small wooden base on its bottom and attached to the flange with nuts and bolts.

Installation

There aren't any tricks to installing a mounted mailbox on a wooden post—a posthole digger and some elbow grease is about all it takes. Once you've chosen the curb- or roadside location for your mailbox, use the posthole digger to dig a hole 2 to 3 feet (60 to 90 cm) deep and a few inches larger than the dimensions of your post. Insert the post in the hole, then backfill the removed earth around the post in the hole and tamp it until the post is secure. For greater stability (or for heavier homemade boxes), you can mix and pour a small amount of concrete around the bottom of the post once it is set in the hole, then backfill with earth once the concrete has set.

If you use a metal pipe as a post, you may not need to do anything more than pound it into the earth in the spot you've picked. If the soil is rocky, though, use the method described above to ensure a sound installation.

Postal Service Requirements

Last but certainly not least, make sure that your mailbox and its mounting and installation will satisfy the postal service. The best way to ensure that your mailbox and its accoutrements and installation comply with codes is to contact your local post office and get the information straight from the source. In the meantime, here are some basic rules and regulations to use as a guide.

Mailbox Construction

- Mailboxes may be made from plastic, wood, or metal; any material that normally sustains a flame must be self-extinguishing.

- The mailbox must not contain any transparent material.

- The mailbox must be weather-tight, with all seams and joints tight enough so that mail is not lost or damaged. It must be safe for both you and the postal delivery worker to use, with no sharp edges, burrs, or projections of any kind which might cause harm to the user.

- Curbside mailboxes must be designed so that all mail can be inserted and retrieved horizontally (i.e., the longest axis of the mailbox must be horizontal). The bottom of the mailbox must not include a lip or protrusion that might restrict the mail being pulled straight out of the box.

- The mailbox door must open and close easily, and remain securely shut when closed. (No spring-loaded mailbox doors! Magnetic door latches are fine, as long as they keep the door properly closed.) You can put a second door on the back of the mailbox to avoid stepping into the road to retrieve your mail, but this door must comply with the same regulations as the front door and not interfere with the operation of the front door.

Mailbox Markings and Decoration

- Your name may be on the mailbox.

- If you have a house or box number, the number must be in a color that contrasts with the mailbox; be at least an inch (2.5 cm) high; and be neat, well defined, and easy to read.

- Any names or numbers on the mailbox must be on the side of the mailbox that is visible to the mail carrier from his or her approach.

- The mailbox can be any color that is clearly visible in its surrounding environment (if you live at the North Pole, don't paint your mailbox white!).

- All finish coatings (paint, varnish, or other) must be free from flaking, peeling, and cracking.

- Mirror-like finishes or coatings on large flat areas of the box should be avoided. When hit by the sun or vehicle lights, they may cause reflected glares that can prove dangerous to oncoming or passing motorists.

Mailbox Flags

- The mailbox flag must be easy for the mail carrier to see and reach. It must be on the right side of the box as you face the box from the road.

- When raised, at least 4 square inches (10 cm) of the flag must be visible above the top of the mailbox, and it must project at least 2 inches (5 cm) above the top of the box; the centerline of the flag should not be more than 2 inches (5 cm) from the front of the mailbox. When lowered, no portion of the flag should be visible above the top of the box.

- The flag may be any color that contrasts with the color of the mailbox except green, brown, and white (trees, earth, and snow!); the color of the flag should not be repeated anywhere else on the mailbox.

- The flag may incorporate a self-lowering feature that automatically drops to the lowered position when the door is opened.

Mailbox Mounts

- The bottom of the mailbox should be 3½ to 4 feet (105 to 120 cm) above the road. The mailbox itself should not project into the road or street.

- No part of the mounting apparatus should project beyond the front or rear of the mounted box, or interfere with the operation of the door or doors.

- Large mailbox supports that, if struck by a vehicle, could damage the vehicle and/or cause injuries to passengers should be avoided. The ideal support is an assemblage that will bend or fall away when struck by a vehicle. (A 4- x 4-inch [10 x 10 cm] wooden post, or 2-inch-diameter [5 cm] steel or aluminum pipe, buried no deeper than 24 inches [60 cm] in the ground, is recommended.)

- The mailbox may be attached to a movable or fixed arm.

- The post may not represent effigies or caricatures that might disparage or ridicule any person.

DESIGNER
JEAN TOMASO MOORE

CHAPTER **2** Simple Contemporary Solutions

Harlequin Pastels

THOUGH it may call to mind the antics of the royal court jester, there's nothing fool-ish about this mailbox's subtle sherbert hues and distinctive diamond pattern. Whether you go with this designer's wonderful colors or switch them to complement your house or apartment, you'll be rewarded with a fantastic addition to any landscape.

☛ Materials

Unpainted metal post-mount mailbox

Primer paint

Acrylic spray paint in tan-green, blue-green, light green, and purple, or other colors of choice

Diamond-shaped stencil, 3 x 5½ inches (7.5 x 13.8 cm), or blank plastic/acrylic for making stencil, at least 5 x 8 inches (12.5 x 20 cm)

Paper

Clear acrylic spray sealer

☛ Tools

Sandpaper

Cloth or rag (to remove dust)

Tape measure

Pencil

Framing square or ruler

Masking tape

Utility or craft knife (if you cut your own stencil)

Painter's tape

Drop cloth

Paint brush

Steel wool cleaning pad (for cleaning the stencil between paintings)

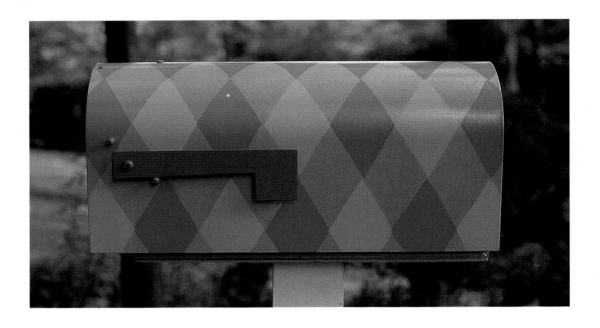

☞ Instructions

1 With sandpaper, slightly refine and smooth the surface of the mailbox. Wipe away the dust, and then apply one coat of primer. Allow this to dry completely.

2 Spray paint the entire mailbox tan-green (or, if you've opted for other hues, the darkest color in your palette); allow the paint to dry to the touch.

3 Use the tape measure to find the center point on the top of the mailbox, and mark this point lightly in pencil. Letting this center point serve as a guide, use the framing square or ruler and pencil to draw a line along the length of the top of the mailbox. This will help you line up the first row of diamonds in the pattern.

4 If you can't find a precut diamond stencil or template, you can cut your own using the blank stencil acrylic. First, draw the design in pencil on paper as follows: Draw a 3-inch (7.5 cm) line and mark its center point. Using the framing square, draw a 5½-inch (13.8 cm) line at a right angle to the first line, with its midpoint positioned on the midpoint of the first line. Connect the lines from endpoint to endpoint to finish the design.

5 Place the paper template on a protected flat surface and tape it down. Lay the blank stencil over the drawing and secure the two with masking tape. Use the craft or utility knife to firmly and smoothly cut out the stencil. Remove the tape, and your stencil is ready to use.

6 Center and position the stencil over the marked center point on top of the mailbox and tape it down with painter's tape. Cover the entire box (except for the open stencil area) with a drop cloth.

7 Spray the stencilled area blue-green (or the second color you've chosen). Let the paint dry thoroughly, then carefully remove the tape and clean the stencil with the dry steel wool cleaning pad.

8 Continuing to use the center line as a guide, lay the stencil down adjacent to the diamond shape you painted in step 7. Follow the instructions in step 7 to complete this diamond shape, then continue repeating this process until you've completed a row of painted diamonds along the length of the top of the mailbox.

9 When the first row of diamonds is complete, start a row immediately underneath, with the upper points of those diamonds touching the lower points of the top row. Work from the center outward, alternating blue-green with light green (or whichever second and third colors you've opted for). The original base coat (this designer's tan-green) will become part of the pattern.

10 Continue stencilling, adding rows on both sides and, if you wish, the front and back, until the box's overall harlequin pattern is complete. Allow the paint to dry completely.

11 Spray a coat of acrylic sealer over the entire box, and allow it to dry thoroughly before handling the box.

12 Spray paint the flag purple (or your desired fourth color). Let it dry thoroughly and apply a coat of acrylic spray sealer. Once the flag is completely dry, attach it to the box. Be sure to wait until all paint and acrylic sealer on the mailbox is dry to the touch before mounting your mailbox.

FREE HOME DELIVERY

The morning of October 1, 1874, marked the start of free home mail delivery for the citizens of Montreal, the first city in Canada to enjoy such a luxury. The new mail system revolutionized Montreal's postal service, combining home delivery with the collection of mail from the city's 30 mailboxes. Not only did the novel operations provide more Canadians the opportunity to become postal workers—the number of letter carriers in Quebec rose from 24 to 45 in the same year—but it inspired Canada's other main cities to update their postal services as well.

By 1875, nearly all the country's large cities had adopted free home delivery. Just as the new trend gained popularity in the rest of the country, however, Montrealers decided the post office promised more fun, after all. Just six years after Montreal home delivery began, letter carriers deposited a mere three out of 20 letters at the city's front doors; the rest remained at the post office, where folks enjoyed an excuse for a bit of company and a chat while picking up the mail.

DESIGNER
SHELLEY LOWELL

CHAPTER **2**
Simple Contemporary Solutions

Airmail Whimsy

THIS delightful aviation-theme mailbox is also delightfully easy to create. There's no guarantee that an airmail mailbox will make all of your mail arrive faster, but there's nothing wrong with positive thinking!

☛ Materials

White metal mailbox with smooth finish

Exterior paint in white and light blue

3 toy airplanes, approximately 4 inches (10 cm) long*

Paint for model planes in red, orange, royal blue, green, silver, black, or other colors of your choice

☛ Tools

Sea sponges

Paint brushes

Pencil

Craft knife or straight edged razor

1 small sheet of medium-grit sandpaper

Epoxy glue

Masking tape

__Note:__ Model airplanes can be found in a hobby shop or toy store.

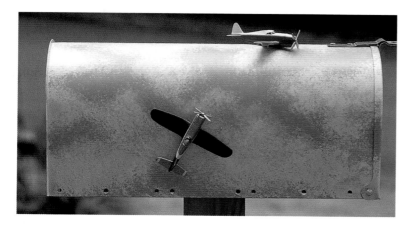

☛ Instructions

1 If necessary, prepare the surface of the mailbox according to instructions on paint containers.

2 Using one of the sponges, sponge light blue paint onto the mailbox, leaving some areas open for clouds. Let the paint dry completely.

3 Once the blue paint is dry, use a clean sponge to apply the white paint in the open areas to simulate clouds. If you want to experiment with different looks, you can go back and forth between white and blue until you achieve the cloud formations you want. Just be sure to let the paint dry between each color.

4 If your planes have wheels or other parts underneath, cut or pull these parts off. Then paint the planes in desired colors and designs, and allow them to dry completely.

5 Decide where you want the planes to go on the mailbox (this designer placed one plane on each side and one on top). When you know where you want them, use the pencil to mark the places where the planes will make contact with the mailbox surface.

6 Using the craft knife (or any straight-edged razor), scrape the paint off of these spots. This is where you will apply glue to the box.

7 Use the sandpaper to sand the paint off the areas of the planes which will make contact with the mailbox.

8 Mix enough epoxy glue for one plane. Paste the first plane onto the mailbox, and then tape the plane in place with masking tape. Allow the glue to set (this takes approximately 12 to 24 hours), and then remove the tape. Turn the mailbox onto another side and repeat the process. You will mix a new batch of epoxy for each plane. When doing the third side (where there will be a plane already glued to the opposite side), use a large book or books to support the box, allowing the already attached plane to hang free.

9 After the glue sets on the last plane, let the paint cure for the amount of time recommended on the paint containers before putting your handiwork outside.

10 Attach the flag according to the manufacturer's instructions, and proudly put your mailbox outside to receive mail!

DESIGNER
JEAN TOMASO MOORE

CHAPTER
2
Simple Contemporary Solutions

Fresh & Breezy Lace

OLD world meets new in this mailbox's mix of clean, contemporary tones and quaint lace pattern. It adds a one-of-a-kind modest charm to any rural or suburban setting.

"The present letter is a very long one, simply because I had no leisure to make it shorter."

—Blaise Pascal
from *Pensées*,
The Provincial Letters

☞ Materials

White metal post-mount mailbox
with smooth surface

1 or 2 brown paper shopping bags

An old lace tablecloth or piece of
lace with an interesting pattern*

Drop cloth or old newspapers

2 cans of fast-drying glossy
latex enamel spray paint
(1 blue-green, 1 medium purple)

Clear acrylic spray sealer

☞ Tools

Scissors

Pencil

Masking tape

*Note: *You'll use whichever cloth
with lace pattern you choose as a
stencil, spray painting over it, so buy
one that can be thrown away after-
ward. Flea markets and yard sales
are the best sources for inexpen-
sive cloths with attractive and often
unusual lace designs. Don't forget
to measure the cloth before purchasing it, to make sure it's large
enough to cover the main body of
the box.*

☞ Instructions

1 Start by using scissors, the pencil, and the brown paper bag to
make a paper template of the mailbox's exterior surfaces. Cut down
the center of the side of a paper bag
and continue the cut line along the
bag's bottom so that the bag is
deconstructed into a single layer.

Wrap the bag around the main body
of the mailbox (the sides and arced
top) and mark with a pencil where
excess bag should be trimmed; cut
along these lines so that the paper
template matches the measurements of the box. Use the leftover
pieces of bag in the same manner
to create to-size templates of the
door and back end of the mailbox.
For now, set aside the template for
the main body. With masking tape,
attach the templates for the front
and back ends to the mailbox, making sure the tape does not overlap
onto the sides or top of the box.

2 Select the lace cloth you have
chosen, and experiment with
different placements of the cloth
on the main body of the mailbox to
find the orientation that allows the
most attractive, uniform design.
When you're satisfied with its position, use masking tape to secure
one end of the cloth to the underside of the mailbox, then wrap the
lace cloth up the side, around the
top, and down the other side of the
mailbox. Secure the cloth to the
bottom of the box on the other side
with tape. Remember, you are using
the lace as a stencil; make sure the
cloth is wrapped evenly—and fairly
tightly, with no wrinkles—around
the box, to avoid irregularities on the
box itself after you've spray-painted
to achieve the painted lace design.

3 Spread out the drop cloth or
old newspapers on the floor

or work surface, and place the cloth-
covered mailbox on top. With a
sweeping motion, spray paint the
body of the box blue-green, covering all of the lace's open cutwork
areas. Allow the paint to dry for 15
or so minutes, then gently peel the
lace off the box.

4 Position and tape the template
you created in step 1 for the
box's main body so that all areas
spray painted with the lace design
are covered. Using the same piece
of lace, experiment as you did in
step 2 to find the best position in
which to attach the lace as stencil
to the back end of the box. Tape the
cloth in place, and spray paint this
end blue-green. When the paint is
dry, remove the lace. Repeat this
process on the front (door) end of
the box. Remove the template from
the main body and allow the painted
mailbox to dry overnight.

5 Spray one or two light coats of
clear acrylic sealer over the
entire box, allowing each coat to dry
completely.

6 Spray paint the door clasp
and screws for the front of
the box blue-green, and the flag
purple. When these pieces are
completely dry, apply one or two
coats of clear acrylic spray sealer,
and allow to dry. Follow the manufacturer's instructions to attach
them to the box. Mount the mailbox and enjoy!

Festive Geometries

DESIGNER
ELLEN ZAHOREC

EVEN if your day's postal intake is nothing but bills and circulars, the trip to this mailbox is sure to paste an ear-to-ear grin on your face. Its offbeat design and melange of berry and citrus hues combine for a look that's stylish and spunky.

☛ Materials

White metal post-mount mailbox with smooth surface

Indoor/outdoor acrylic or enamel spray paint in hot pink, blue-green, gold, and different shades of light green

Broad-tipped enamel paint marker pens in bright blue, bright pink, orange, purple, and black

Clear acrylic spray sealer

☛ Tools

Masking tape

Ruler (optional)

☛ Instructions

1 Starting along the bottom edge of one side of the box, use long strips of masking tape to create crisscross patterns that arc over the box top and end along the bottom edge of the other side of the box. Three or four evenly spaced crisscross patterns will work well for a standard-sized mailbox. Use shorter strips to make abstract designs with intersecting lines on the front and back of the box. Play with the placement of the strips of tape until you find a pattern you like.

2 Alternating hot pink, blue-green, gold, and different shades of light green to create a pleasing overall color scheme, spray paint with one light coat each unmasked, roughly diamond-shaped space. Allow the paint to dry thoroughly, then remove the masking tape.

3 With your black enamel marker, draw simple, regularly spaced triangles on the crisscrossing white surface area. Use a bright blue marker to draw lines closely around different sides of the black triangles. (These need not create actual borders or outlines; a little randomness in their placement will give a more artistic effect.)

4 Finish decorating the box by using the markers to make dots, dashes, triangles, and small designs incorporating all three elements, in different color combinations. This designer incorporated solid triangles outlined in a second color, linked and surrounded by rows and random arrangements of dots in a third hue; triangle outlines bordered by small dashes and dots in contrasting colors; and designs merging the two patterns. Follow her lead and use the photograph as a guide, or invent your own abstract geometric motifs.

5 Allow the finished mailbox to dry overnight, then apply one or two coats of acrylic sealer and allow the box to dry completely. Attach the flag according to manufacturer's instructions, then mount the mailboxbox for use.

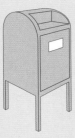

Mail Note...

Letters in Literature

In the age of electronic communication, letter writing is all but a lost art. No matter how much it may disappear from daily life, though, there will always be epistolary novels—works written in the form of a series of letters—to return to when your heart and soul yearn for that feeling nothing but an old-fashioned letter can deliver (even if you have to find them on the internet and read them on your computer screen). If you're in the mood to take one in while you're in mailbox mode, here's a sampling of some great ones old and new from the literary archives:

- *Pamela and Clarissa*, by Samuel Richardson
- *Les Liaisons Dangereuses*, by Pierre Choderlos de Laclos
- *La Nouvelle Heloise*, by Jean Jacques Rousseau
- *The Color Purple*, by Alice Walker
- *The Mixquiahala Letters*, by Ana Castillo
- *Another Pamela*, by Upton Sinclair
- *S.*, by John Updike
- *Letters*, by John Barth
- *Daddy-Long-Legs*, by Jean Webster
- *Fair and Tender Ladies*, by Lee Smith
- *The Griffin & Sabine Trilogy: Sabine's Notebook*, *The Golden Mean*, and *Griffin & Sabine*, by Nick Bantock

Pink & White Dogwood

DESIGNER
MELISSA STOWERS

CHAPTER **2** Simple Contemporary Solutions

THERE aren't many sights more lovely than a dogwood tree in blossom in the springtime. With this beautifully decorated mailbox, you can have the pleasure of seeing delicate dogwood blooms year round—and of making a mailbox whose graceful look will quietly stand apart from those of others on your street.

☛ Materials

Dogwood patterns (see figures 1 and 2 on page 123)

White metal post-mount mailbox

White graphite paper

2 square paintbrushes (1 medium, 1 small)

Acrylic paints in deep pink, white, dark brown, bright yellow, bright green, and dark green

1 long liner brush

Scrap paper

☛ Tools

Scissors or craft knife

Clear tape

Pencil

Clear acrylic spray sealer

☛ Instructions

1 Enlarge, by photocopying to 200 percent or to the desired size, the designs in figures 1 and 2 on page 123. Cut out the designs with scissors or a craft knife.

2 Following the photograph or inventing your own arrangement, determine placement positions on the mailbox for different designs. You'll probably want to use the design with multiple blossoms on the side of the mailbox without the flag, and the single blossom clusters on the side including the flag. Tape the graphite paper to the mailbox over the placement points, then tape the design cutouts over the graphite paper in the spots you've chosen. Firmly trace over the designs with a pencil. (You can,

of course, also freehand draw the dogwood designs onto the mailbox if you choose.) Remove the taped design cutouts and graphite paper.

3 Now you're ready to paint the dogwood blossoms. Select the medium, square paintbrush and the pink and white paints. Dip the brush in the paints so that one half of the bristles are covered verti-

cally with pink paint, and the other half with white. Apply the paint to one of the dogwood petals, making a long comma stroke first on one side of the petal, then the other. These strokes may meet in the center of the petal; if not, paint another stroke to fill in the center. Repeat this process on all the remaining petals, and allow the painted petals to dry thoroughly.

4 To paint the leaves, again use the medium, square brush, this time with the bristles dipped in a combination of bright yellow and bright and dark green paints. (Be sure to rinse the paintbrush thoroughly in water between uses.) Begin to create one leaf close to the painted blossom. Press the brush down and drag it gently away from the blossom with a "squiggly" motion, lifting the brush to apply the paint more narrowly near the point of the leaf; repeat this process on the other side of the leaf. (For tiny leaves, you'll only need to make a single stroke.) Continue this technique until all the leaves are painted, then allow the paint to dry to the touch.

5 Dip the long liner brush in brown paint and make long lines to create branches linking the blossoms and leaves as shown. Don't worry about making straight lines—branches crook and bend! Let the paint flow naturally. Again, let the paint dry completely before proceeding.

6 Before painting the centers of the dogwood flowers, practice on scrap paper stippling green, yellow, brown, and white paint to create small circles. To do this, use the small brush or liner brush dipped in very sparing amounts of green and brown paint to dab at the paper so the paint forms a rough circle. Repeat this process with the brush dipped in yellow paint, then finish up with a few white dots for the finished look. When you're comfortable with your execution of the technique, use it to create the dogwood centers on the mailbox itself.

7 The last painting step is to use the long liner brush to add highlights and outlines to the flowers, leaves, and branches. Following the photograph to locate highlight lines and outlines, use brown paint to create the indentations for dogwood blossoms and a mix of white and pink to outline the blossoms; white paint to highlight branches; and white or yellow mixed with a little bright or dark green to highlight leaves. If you like, you can also use a mixture of green and yellow paint to add a few "squiggle" marks for vines.

8 Allow the finished design to dry for 24 hours, then spray the mailbox with a coat of clear acrylic to seal the painted design. Allow the acrylic to dry, then attach the flag and hardware and mount your mailbox.

TWO LETTER CARRIERS POSE WITH THEIR PARCEL POST WAGONS, filled to the brim with the day's deliveries. COURTESY OF THE U.S. POSTAL SERVICE.

DESIGNER
BETH PALMER

CHAPTER 2
Simple Contemporary Solutions

Spring Garden

THIS mailbox decoration's floral explosion will put spring in your heart and a spring in your step every time you meander out to gather your mail. It's perfect for the horticulturally inclined, whether you're an avid gardener or just happen to love bountiful flora.

☛ Materials

White metal post- or wall-mount mailbox

Sea sponges

Acrylic paint in a variety of colors including light green, medium green, dark green, beige (optional), and an assortment of floral hues (red, yellow, purple, lavender, pink, aqua, etc.)

Container for water

White graphite paper

Clear acrylic spray sealer

☛ Tools

Clear tape

Pencil

Assortment of small paintbrushes

☛ Instructions

1 Using a sea sponge, sponge dark green onto the areas of the mailbox you plan to cover with leaves and flowers. Sponge lightly, so that some of the white of the mailbox surface still shows through, and don't forget the back and front of the mailbox! Let the paint dry completely.

2 Using a clean sea sponge, sponge a coat of medium green onto the same areas, being sure to let areas of dark green show through. Allow to dry, then repeat this process with a clean sponge and the light green, leaving some areas of both dark and medium green visible. Allow the paint to dry to the touch before proceeding.

3 You're now ready to start painting the flowers. You can do this freehand or use the patterns provided in figure 3 on page 121. To use the patterns, enlarge them by photocopying to desired sizes, then cut them out. Tape the graphite paper to the mailbox, then tape the flower designs onto the graphite paper in desired locations. Firmly trace over the designs with the pencil, then remove the graphite paper.

4 When you're ready to start painting, begin with the larger flowers (such as the sunflowers on this mailbox), starting about 3 inches (7.5 cm) in from the front of the box and placing them 3 to 5 inches (7.5 to 12.5 cm) apart and 2 to 3 inches (5 to 7.5 cm) up or down from each other. Next, move on to the medium-sized flowers, placing these randomly between and around the larger flowers, and occasionally overlapping them. Fill in your painted garden with the smaller flowers, again occasionally overlapping with the other blooms to give the illusion of depth in your design.

5 Put the finishing touches on your mailbox by adding leaves and vines to accent the flowers. Use the same assortment of green paints you used for sponge painting the background, and paint leaves around and among the flowers, filling in and overlapping as you go. Include some vines growing up from the bottom of the mailbox to enhance the illusion of depth. Add some clumps of baby's breath by sponging with beige paint, if desired. Again, don't forget the back and front of the mailbox. Allow the paint to dry overnight.

6 Seal the entire mailbox with acrylic sealer, and allow it to dry completely. Attach the hardware and flag then mount the mailbox.

Rustic Birch

DESIGNER
PEGGY HAYES

CHAPTER 3
Wall-Mount Alternatives

THIS easy-to-make piece is a perfect rustic complement for a log cabin or summer retreat, and can lend a woodsy touch to a suburban home. It's better to buy your bark, rather than strip it from unsuspecting trees; birch bark can be found in most craft supply stores.

☛ Materials

4-foot-length (1.23 m) of 1 x 12 (1.9 x 28.1 cm) pine stock

Piece of plywood, 10 x 3 inches (25 x 7.5 cm)

1¼-inch (3.1 cm) screws

2 brass hinges, 2¾ inches (6.9 cm), with screws

Acrylic paint in gray and red

1 washer, ⅛ inch (3 mm)

1 flat washer

Wood glue or adhesive

Birch bark

Plastic wrap

3-inch (7.5 cm) twig

2 large flat brass ring hangers

☛ Tools

Circular saw or jigsaw

Screwdriver

Drill with ⅛-inch (3 mm) drill bit

Paint brush

Disposable paint brush (for applying glue)

☛ Cut List

DESC	QTY	MATERIAL	DIMENSIONS
Front	1	1 x 12 pine (1.9 x 29 cm)	$6\frac{3}{8}$ x $9\frac{3}{4}$ inches (15.9 x 24.4 cm)
Back	1	1 x 12 pine (1.9 x 29 cm)	$6\frac{3}{8}$ x $12\frac{7}{8}$ inches (15.9 x 32.2 cm)
Sides	2	1 x 12 pine (1.9 x 29 cm)	3 x $12\frac{7}{8}$ inches (7.5 x 32.2 cm)
Bottom	1	1 x 12 pine (1.9 x 29 cm)	3 x 5 inches (7.5 x 12.5 cm)
Top	1	1 x 12 pine (1.9 x 29 cm)	$6\frac{3}{8}$ x $12\frac{7}{8}$ inches (15.9 x 32.2 cm)
Flag	1	exterior grade plywood	$2\frac{1}{4}$ x $8\frac{1}{4}$ inches (5.6 x 20.6 cm)

(**Note**: for additional guidance in constructing the Rustic Birch mailbox, refer to figures 2 through 4 on page 117.)

☛ Instructions

1 With the circular saw or jigsaw, cut the top edge of the front piece to a 45° bevel. Cut the two side pieces to a 45° angle. (See figures 4 and 3, page 117.)

2 Use the jigsaw to cut the flag out of the plywood, according to the pattern shown in figure 2, page 117.

3 Fit the front, sides, back, and bottom together, and assemble them so that the edges of the front and back pieces are flush with the faces of the side pieces, using ¼-inch (3.1 cm) screws. (It may help to use the drill to start the screw holes, in which case use the ⅛-inch [3mm] bit.) Countersink the screws.

4 Attach the top piece using the two hinges screwed to the inner surfaces of the top and back.

5 Paint the flag, using gray or another desired color for the stem and red for the flag itself. Allow the paint to dry completely.

6 Use the drill and 1/8-inch (3mm) bit to bore a small hole, centered 1/2 inch (1.3cm) from the non-flag end, in the flag's stem. On the left-hand side of the mailbox, measure 9 7/8 inches (24.7cm) up from the bottom of the mailbox and 2 1/2 inches (6.25cm) from the back. Attach the flag at the point where the two measurements meet by placing the 1/8-inch (3mm) washer under the hole in the stem, then placing the flag against the mailbox, and finally placing the flat washer on top of the hole in the stem. Screw the flag stem into the side of the box so that it is tight enough to be secure, but loose enough that it can be raised and lowered.

7 Using the disposable brush, spread a thin, even layer of glue over the surface of one side of the mailbox. Starting at the top or bottom, position and gently press into the glue pieces of birch bark, arranging and layering them for a pleasing effect, until the glued surface is covered. Lay the mailbox on a table or work surface with the bark-covered-side face up, cover the bark with a sheet of plastic wrap to protect it, and weight it down with a brick or other heavy object. Allow the glued bark to thoroughly set, then repeat the above process on the other three sides of the mailbox.

8 Using the wood glue, glue the twig centered and about 1/4 inch (6mm) from the bottom edge onto the top piece; this will serve as the mailbox's handle. Then follow the directions in step 7 to cover the top of the box with birch bark.

9 Center and screw the two large brass hangers onto the back of the box, and mount it on the wall.

IN 1922, THE GEHRING MAIL DISTRIBUTING MACHINE was briefly tested at the Washington, D.C., post office. The machine showed promise: Five clerks sitting at keyboards could sort mail to 120 separations—twice the number possible when using manual sorting cases. Yet as America turned its head toward infinitely more pressing concerns—the Great Depression and World War II—mail processing technology progressed little in the ensuing decades. Not until the 1950s would a non-manual sorting system become a viable reality.

COURTESY OF THE U.S. POSTAL SERVICE.

Mail Note...

When Musical Notes and Love Notes Meet

There's probably not a soul among us who hasn't pined for a lost love when listening to songs on the radio or happily hummed an anticipatory tune while eagerly awaiting a letter from a loved one far away. No surprise, then, that a bevy of musicians and entertainers have written and performed songs on the joys, melancholies, and—in the case of "Dear John" and "Dear Jane" letters— sometimes down-right agonies of love letters sent and received. Most notably popularized in the 1950s, the genre of songs devoted to epistles includes among its ranks the following tunes from different decades:

Please, Mr Postman, by The Marvelettes

Return to Sender, words and music by Otis Blackwell and Winfield Scott, performed by Elvis Presley

The Letter, by The Boxtops

P.S. I Love You, by the Beatles

From Me to You, by the Beatles

Hello Mudduh, Hello Fadduh (A Letter from Camp), written by Allan Sherman and Louis Bush, performed by Allan Sherman

Signed, Sealed, Delivered, I'm Yours, by Stevie Wonder

In Your Letter, REO Speedwagon

Take a Letter, Maria, written by R.B. Greaves, performed by Gary Puckett and the Union Gap

Tear-Stained Letter, written by Richard John Thompson, performed by Reilly and Maloney

Faux Stone Mosaic

MAKING this simple mailbox mosaic is a great way to try your hand at the craft and get a stunning mailbox to boot. Its natural slate tones and tidy design give it an understated, classic look that satisfies a wide range of tastes.

DESIGNER **TAMARA MILLER**

CHAPTER 3 Wall-Mount Alternatives

☞ Materials

4 to 5 unglazed slate-gray ceramic tiles, 4 x 4 inches (10 x 10 cm)

5 unglazed ceramic tiles (1 each in dark, light, and medium beige; 1 purple-gray; and 1 light green-gray [or other natural shades of your choice]), each 4 x 4 inches (10 x 10 cm)

1 sheet of paper, 8½ x 11 inches (21.3 x 27.5 cm)

Tile adhesive

Black metal wall-mount mailbox, 3 x 5 x 15 inches (7.5 x 12.5 x 37.5 cm)

1 cup (.24 L) unsanded grout

Water

☞ Tools

Old large bath towel

Rubber mallet

Protective eye wear

Ruler

Pencil

¼ inch (6 mm) V-notch ceramic trowel

Small plastic container for mixing grout

Sponge or damp cloth

Float or spatula

Dry cloth

☞ Instructions

1 Gather all your tiles and wrap them in an old towel. Working on a cement driveway or similarly hard surface, use the rubber mallet to pound on the wrapped tiles and break them into smaller pieces. Remember to wear protective eye gear during this step and to be careful handling the broken pieces to avoid getting nicks or cuts on your hands.

2 On the scrap piece of paper, use a ruler and pencil to measure and mark a 15- x 5-inch (37.5 x 12.5 cm) rectangle; this will serve as a template as you experiment with the tile pieces to devise the best mosaic design. Lay the paper on a work table or other flat surface and, following the photograph or inventing your own design, arrange the shards of broken tile at least ⅛ to ¼ inch (3 to 6 mm) apart within the template's parameters to find the overall pattern and tile positions that look best. Even if you decide to create an abstract design with randomly placed shards of tile, it's a good idea to experiment with

them to get a feeling for how much space you have to work with and how they will fit together.

3 Apply the tile adhesive to the mailbox according to the manufacturer's instructions, then use the trowel to make lines in the adhesive (these lines will help the tile stick to the mailbox surface). Place the tiles on the adhesive in the design you've created. Allow the adhesive to set for at least 24 hours, or until it is completely dry.

4 In the plastic container, mix the grout with water until it reaches the consistency of toothpaste. Use the float or spatula to spread the grout across the tiles, making sure to get grout in all the cracks between tiles, until the surface is smooth and even. Use a damp cloth to clean up around the tiles as you grout. Let the grout dry for 24 hours, then use a dry cloth to buff the surfaces of the tiles. Make sure all grout and adhesive on the mailbox is completely dry before mounting your mailbox.

Eye-Catching
(Fly-Catching!)
Frog & Beads

A GREAT offbeat touch for urban or neighborhood suburban abodes, this cool and easy-to-create mailbox lets you receive your mail in fun and quirky style. A quick trip to the hobby or toy and craft store, a few hours, and it's ready to hang!

☞ Materials

2 bright green rubber frogs
   (1 small, 1 large)

Blue (or color of your choice)
   metal wall-mount mailbox

Medium-gauge wire
   (easily bendable)

20 glass beads with large holes

2 silver-gray rubber flies,
   extra small

☞ Tools

Marker

Drill with bit that will
   accommodate wire gauge

Needle-nose pliers

☛ Instructions

1 Select the large frog and position it diagonally on the front of the mailbox, with its feet at the lower left-hand corner and its head pointing toward the top right-hand corner. With a marker, make four dots on the mailbox where the frog meets the surface: one behind each front leg, and one in front of each back leg. Position the smaller frog on the mailbox lid as shown in the photograph or as you prefer, and mark a small dot just behind each of its two front legs. Try to position the dots so that they will be hidden beneath the frog bodies.

2 Drill holes in the mailbox at each of the marked points; drill carefully, so as not to cause the box to buckle during drilling.

3 Cut a piece of wire sufficiently long to be threaded down through one of the holes behind the large frog's front legs, around the underside of the mailbox front, up through the hole on the other side, and around the frog's body, with enough extra length to string beads and bend curlicue designs. Do the same for the two holes just in front of the large frog's hind legs.

4 Thread the wire through the top drilled holes so that you end up with both loose ends on top of the box. Place the frog in its designated position, twist the loose strands together over its body to secure it to the box, and thread beads onto the remaining wire. Bend or twist the wire as desired, being careful not to crush the glass beads, and use the needle nose pliers to form curlicues at the ends of the wire—this will keep the beads from slipping off, and will also protect hands from sharp wire ends.

5 Repeat the process described in steps 3 and 4 to attach the smaller frog to the lid of the mailbox and bead the securing wire.

6 Position rubber or plastic flies as pictured or in an arrangement that pleases you, then mark and drill a single hole where the center of each insect meets the mailbox surface. Cut a short length of wire about 2 to 2½ inches (5 to 6.3 cm) long, reposition the insect over the hole, and from the underside of the mailbox front, thread the wire through the hole and rubber insect. Leave approximately ½ inch (1.3 cm) of wire on the underside of the mailbox, thread one small bead onto the wire and flush with the underside; use the needle nose pliers to curve the wire around the bead to secure the wire to the box. Last, thread a bead onto the outside wire so that it is flush with the fly or other insect, and use needle-nose pliers to bend the extra wire into a pretty curlicue design.

Dramatic Doodles

☛ Materials

A white metal mailbox with smooth surface (wall- or post-mount boxes will work equally well)

Scrap paper for practice doodles (optional)

Black acrylic or enamel paint (or color of your choice)

Clear acrylic spray sealer

☛ Tools

Pencil with eraser

Paintbrush (small)

Plastic container (for water, to clean brush while working)

(**Note:** *The freehand doodling approach adds fun and spontaneity to making this project, but the simple technique of using pencil and marker is easily adapted for use with pictorial or letter stencils, allowing you to use favorite images or personalized designs with a more refined look.*)

WHO among us hasn't absent-mindedly created an abstract mini-masterpiece with ballpoint pen and paper while chatting on the phone? Making this striking, zesty mailbox is as much fun as being greeted by it when you go for the mail. Not only can you can get your frustrations out constructively, with almost no materials you wind up with a unique accent for your porch!

☞ Instructions

1 Start by drawing in pencil your doodle or other pattern on the box. Since doodles are by their nature individualized, your design will differ from the one shown. You may have a favorite doodle stashed away somewhere that you can replicate to start your design off, or you can practice drawing different shapes and figures on scrap paper to get your "doodle momentum" going. The best way to proceed is to create a central image or images and an outer or border image or pattern on the surface area you're working on (front, back, sides, or top), then fill in spaces between with shapes and lines that echo or complement each other. Concentric circles, plain or adorned zigzag lines, simple floral motifs, diamonds and other geometric shapes such as this designer used work well together, are easy to draw, and need not be perfectly executed to look good. Creating your pattern in pencil first lets you experiment with different combinations, erasing what you don't like or doesn't work, until you find a design you're happy with.

2 When your pencilled doodle "blueprint" is complete, use a small paintbrush to go over all of your pencilled lines with black enamel or acrylic paint (or the color you prefer). Work on one side at a time, allowing each to dry to the touch before starting a next.

3 If your mailbox will be exposed to the elements, apply one to two coats of acrylic sealer and allow it to dry completely before mounting.

WILLIAM "BIG BILL" HOPSON exemplified the tough and ready spirit of early airmail pilots. These adventurous aviators, known for their daredevilry, were so fearless that the U.S. Post Office had to issue a regulation forbidding "riding on the steps, wings, or tail of a flying machine."

COURTESY OF THE U.S. POSTAL SERVICE

Little Country House

DESIGNER
PEGGY HAYES

CHAPTER **3** Wall-Mount Alternatives

THIS easy-to-create mailbox gives a sweet country touch to your house front (or wherever else you may choose to mount it). With a few pieces of wood, a couple colors of paint, and a minimum of time and effort, you'll have a charming little home for your missives and other mail.

☛ Materials

Lumber (see "Cut List")

1¼-inch (3.1 cm) screws

2 brass hinges, 2¾ inch (6.9 cm), with screws

Wood filler

Medium-grade sandpaper

1 washer, ⅛ inch (3 mm)

Flat washer

¾-inch (1.9 cm) wooden square

Acrylic paints in gray, light blue, pink, mauve, red, peach, light and dark green, brown, and white

White paint pen

Acrylic varnish

2 large brass flat ring hangers

☛ Tools

Circular saw or jigsaw

Pencil

Drill with ⅛-inch (3 mm) drill bit and ⅛-inch (3 mm) countersink bit

Screwdriver

Paintbrushes (large, medium, small)

Carbon paper (optional)

☛ Instructions

1 With the circular saw or jigsaw, cut the top edge of the piece of pine for the mailbox front to a 45° bevel. Cut the two pieces of pine for the sides to a 45° angle (see Rustic Birch figures 4 and 3, p. 117, for examples of these cuts).

2 Enlarge by photocopying to 200 percent, or to fit the 13⅞-inch (34.5 cm) mailbox front, the pattern

☛ Cut List

DESC	QTY	MATERIAL	DIMENSIONS
Front	1	1 x 12 pine (1.9 x 29 cm)	6 x 13⅞ inches (15 x 34.5 cm)
Back	1	1 x 12 pine (1.9 x 29 cm)	9 1/16 x 13⅞ inches (22.55 x 34.5 cm)
Sides	2	1 x 12 pine (1.9 x 29 cm)	3 x 9 1/16 inches (7.5 x 22.55 cm)
Top	1	1 x 12 pine (1.9 x 29 cm)	6 x 14 inches (15 x 35 cm)
Bottom	1	1 x 12 pine (1.9 x 29 cm)	3 x 12 5/16 inches (7.5 x 30.1 cm)
Flag stem with flag	1	¼-inch-thick (6 mm) exterior grade plywood	2¼ x 7¼ inches (5.06 x 17.56 cm)

shown in figure 3 on page 120. With a pencil, trace the pattern for the flag stem and flag onto the piece of plywood, then use the saw to cut out the flag stem with flag.

3 Fit the front, sides, back, and bottom together and assemble the box with countersunk 1¼-inch (3.1 cm) screws. You may want to predrill these screw holes with the ⅛-inch (3 mm) bit and countersink bit.

4 Attach the top of the box to the back by screwing the hinges to the inside surfaces of the back and top. Make sure to position and attach the hinges so the top opens and closes freely.

5 Fill in all the screw holes with wood filler. When the filler dries, use the sandpaper to sand it smooth where it meets the wood surface of the mailbox.

6 Using the ⅛-inch (3 mm) bit, drill a small hole in the stem of the flag centered ½ inch (1.3 cm) from the non-flag end. Measure 7¼ inches (18 cm) from the bottom of the mailbox and 1¾ inches (4.4 cm) from the back and, with a pencil, mark the point where the two measurements meet. Attach the flagstem here by placing the ⅛-inch (3-mm) washer under the hole in the stem, then placing the stem against the mailbox, and finally placing the flat washer on top of the hole in the stem. Screw the flag into the side of the box so that it is tight enough to be secure, but still loose enough to move up and down freely.

7 Glue the wooden square to the center of the front edge of the mailbox top to use as a handle.

8 With a medium or large paintbrush, paint the sides, back, bottom, and front of the assembled mailbox and the stem of the flag blue. Paint the top of the mailbox gray, and the flag itself red. Allow all the painted surfaces to dry thoroughly.

Little Country House, *continued*

9 Next, follow the photograph on page 40, or use the pattern provided in figure 3 on page 120 (you can use carbon paper to trace the design onto the mailbox, if you like) and use the small paintbrush and paint pen to paint the house design on the front of your mailbox. Use the white paint pen to outline the door and windows and to fill in the window box shapes at the bottom of each window. Using the traced design as a guide, paint the window shutters and door pink, then fill in the window spaces with gray. Next, carefully go over the thin tree trunks and branches with brown paint. To create the leaves on trees and the greenery in the two window boxes, dip the small brush in green paint (dark green for the window box greenery, and light green and white for the tree leaves) and use a "stippling" technique, making small dots and dabs to make natural leafy shapes and flesh them out. Use this same technique to paint grass along the bottom edge of the mailbox front, and a small tree on each side of the door. Last, paint tiny dots of peach, mauve, and red to create the look of small blooms in the window box greenery. When the design is finished, allow the paint to dry completely.

10 Apply two coats of acrylic varnish to the entire mailbox, allowing the first coat to dry to the touch before applying the second.

11 Screw ring hangers onto the back of the mailbox and mount it on the wall or post of your choice.

Brass & Blooms

DESIGNER **TAMARA MILLER**

CHAPTER **3** Wall-Mount Alternatives

IN just a few quick steps, this elegant mailbox is ready to adorn a porch-front wall or the facade of your home. Plant some bright petunias or a flowering vine with blossoms in your favorite colors for spring, then swap blooms as the months go by for an up-to-the-minute seasonal look.

Materials

Black metal wall-mount mailbox

Flat-back brass planter, approximately 3 x 5½ x 7 inches (7.5 x 12.5 x 17.5 cm)

Brass or brass-plated drawer pull, 1¼ inches (3.1 cm) diameter x 1¼ inches (3.1 cm) long

Plant of choice

Instructions

1 Center the brass planter on the front of the mailbox, and use the marker to label the drilling point.

2 Using the appropriate drill bit for your planter and drawer pull, drill a hole through the mailbox at the marked point. Be careful not to buckle the mailbox while drilling.

3 Instead of using a visible screw to secure the planter to the mailbox, try a decorative drawer pull—hardware and home supply stores, and even antique shops, have a wide array to choose from.

4 Plant flowers or greenery of your choice in the planter. Mount on the wall and enjoy!

Tools

Drill (with bit size appropriate to your planter and drawer pull)

Marker

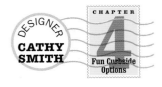

DESIGNER
CATHY SMITH

CHAPTER
4
Fun Curbside Options

WHAT better way to embellish your mailbox than with a sleek and eager leopard ready to pounce on an astronomical bill or two? This fabulous feline may not do away with debt or write your checks for you, but in its setting of exotic flora, it can't help but put a smile on your face no matter what you find in the box.

☛ Materials

White metal post-mount mailbox with smooth surface

Pattern cutouts (see figures, page 115)

5 sheets of fade-resistant colored paper, each 14 x 18 inches (35 x 45 cm): 1 black, 1 purple, 1 orange, 1 green, and 1 yellow

Craft glue

Black acrylic paint

Matte medium

Spray varnish or polyurethane

☛ Tools

Fine sandpaper

Pencil

Craft knife with extra blade

Scissors (small)

Paintbrush (small, flat)

1 or 2 paintbrushes (small, round)

Rubber cutting mat or uncorrugated matboard, at least 16 x 20 inches (40 x 50 cm), or any other smooth, protective cutting surface

☛ Instructions

1 With the fine sandpaper, sand (working in one direction) the mailbox surface to reduce the glossy finish. Dampen a paper towel or cloth and wipe away any paint particles removed by the sanding process.

2 Using the photos on page 44 and 46 as guides, enlarge by photocopying the patterns on page 115 to fit your mailbox. Then trace them onto the sheets of fade-resistant paper so that you have the following: two tall orange grass shapes; two medium-tall green grass shapes; two short purple grass shapes; two extra-short black grass shapes; two black leopard shapes; two yellow leopard shapes; two black tree trunk shapes; and a variety of leaf cluster shapes.

3 Working on the rubber mat or matboard, cut out all the shapes with scissors or a craft knife. Be sure to work on a smooth, protective surface that will not dull the sharp point or blade of the craft knife—avoid working on wood, metal, or other dulling surfaces.

4 Use the flat brush to apply a thin, even layer of craft glue to the back of one of the short black grass shapes, and attach it approximately halfway up one side of the mailbox. Pat the strip down with a clean, damp paper towel or cloth to help it adhere to the mailbox surface. (You will use the process described above to attach all remaining cutouts to the box.) Glue, position, and attach the purple,

green, and orange grass shapes in layers as shown in the photograph, allowing each color to show above the previously placed strip.

5 Select one of the black tree trunk cutouts. Glue and attach it to the side of the box you're working on with the cutout's flat side flush with the door-end of the box, and the branches extending across the side of the box.

6 Select the black leopard cutout and position it on the tree's lower branch with its hind end approximately 1 inch (2.5 cm) away from the point at which the tree's trunk and lower branch intersect. Its nose should be flush with the top of the branch at the other end.

When you've found its proper position, glue and attach it. Position the yellow leopard slightly off-center over the attached black leopard shape, so that a black border shows around the top of the leopard's head and body and slightly on both sides of its hanging tail and paws. Glue and attach it.

7 From a scrap of black paper, cut one isosceles triangle measuring $1/2$ x $1/2$ x $1/4$ inch (1.3 cm x 1.3 cm x 6 mm). From a scrap of green paper, cut a slightly smaller isosceles triangle measuring about $1/4$ x $1/4$ x $1/8$ inch (6 x 6 x 3 mm). Apply a dab of glue to the back of the green triangle, center it over the black triangle so that a thin border of black shows all around it,

and attach it to the black triangle. Position the two-layered triangle eye shape with its short side more or less parallel with the indentation where the leopard's brow and nose meet; glue and attach it to the leopard shape.

8 Use the small round paintbrush and black acrylic paint to paint small, hollow rosette shapes spaced approximately ⅛ inch (3 mm) apart all over the leopard's body.

9 Following the photograph or inventing your own arrangement, position, glue, and attach leaf clusters at the ends of branches and in any other places you like.

10 Repeat steps 4 through 9 on the other side of the mailbox.

11 Use a brush to apply a thin, even layer of matte medium over all areas of the paper design attached to the mailbox surface—but not on the mailbox surface itself. This will seal the applied paper design. Allow the matte medium to dry overnight.

12 With a cloth or damp paper towel, remove any excess glue from the mailbox surface.

13 Spray the mailbox with a coat of polyurethane or clear varnish, and allow it to dry completely. Lightly sand the dried coat of polyurethane or varnish and wipe well to remove dust. Repeat this process, then spray a third, final coat onto the box. Allow the third coat to dry completely before assembling and mounting the mailbox.

UNION ARMY MAIL WAGON DRIVERS maintained exceptional efficiency during the Civil War, despite muddy, often treacherous, and sometimes nearly impassable roads and extreme temperatures. The "traveling post office" they operated sold stamps and collected and distributed correspondence.

COURTESY OF THE LIBRARY OF CONGRESS

DESIGNER
CHA CHA DONAHUE

CHAPTER
4
Fun Curbside Options

Checkers & Cherries

A **NEAT** checkerboard border, ladybug-red polka dots, and a perky cluster of cherries nicely contrast with the black-and-yellow color scheme of this mailbox to give it streamlined flair with just enough whimsy. Easy to put together, it makes a great curbside statement with unconventional panache.

☛ Materials

Unpainted metal post-mount
    mailbox with finely corrugated
    surface

Enamel or acrylic spray paint in
    red, yellow, and black

17 or more ¼-inch (6 mm)
    wooden plugs

Contact cement

Clear silicone sealer

2 tiny screws (no larger than ¼
    inch [6 mm] long with ¼-inch-
    diameter [6 mm] heads)

1 large bunch of wooden fake
    cherries (or 2 small bunches
    wired together to give the
    effect of a single large bunch)

1 strip of black-and-white
    checkerboard self-adhesive
    shelf paper, 21½ x 2½
    inches (53.75 x 6.25 cm)

☛ Tools

Coarse sandpaper

Drill with ¼-inch (6 mm) bit and
    bit to fit screws

Masking tape

Ruler

Screwdriver (small)

Old credit card or rubber spatula

☛ Instructions

1 Lightly sand the exterior surfaces of the mailbox to make
the finish less smooth. This will
allow the paint to better adhere to
the mailbox.

2 With your drill and a ¼-inch
(6 mm) bit, bore holes approximately 4 inches (10 cm) apart in
rows (or the pattern you prefer) on
either side of the mailbox, to accommodate the decorative plugs. (This
designer used seven plugs on the
side of the mailbox that includes the
flag, and 10 on the other, to give a
uniform effect.)

3 Next, spray paint all the plugs
you'll use on the mailbox red,
and stand the mailbox on its end
(door down) and spray paint the end
red. If the mailbox's flag is removable, you can detach it and spray
paint it red, too. Allow the plugs and
end (and flag, if you have removed
and painted it) to dry overnight, or
until they are dry to the touch.

4 When the painted plugs and
mailbox end are thoroughly dry,
stand the box on end with the red
side down and spray paint the door
black. Allow the painted door to dry
overnight or until it is completely dry
to the touch.

5 Loosely mask with masking tape
the painted black and red ends
of the box (also the flag, if it is per-
manently fixed to the box and still
unpainted) so they are covered, but
the tape does not stick to the painted
ends. Spray paint the mailbox yellow.

6 Apply a small amount of contact cement around the neck of
a plug, and insert the plug into one
of the holes you drilled in step 2.
Repeat this process for all the
remaining plugs. When the cement
has fully dried, open the mailbox
and, starting at the back, apply a
thick layer of the silicon sealer to the
back of each plug.

7 On the right side of the front of
the mailbox door, measure in
1¾ inches (4.4 cm) from the side
and 4 inches (10 cm) up from the bottom of the mailbox door, and use your
drill and screw-sized bit to bore a tiny
hole at the point where the two measurements meet. On the left side of
the door, measure in 1½ inches
(3.8 cm) and 2¾ inches (6.9 cm) and
drill a second hole where these measurements intersect. Next, use your
screwdriver to insert a single tiny
screw through each hole from the
back of the door through the front.

8 From your bunch of wooden
cherries, select two at opposite
sides of the bunch; still using the bit
you used in step 7, drill a centered
hole on the side or back of each of
the two cherries, then mount them
onto the screw ends protruding from
the front of the door. Play with
arrangements of the bunch(es) of
hanging cherries until you are
pleased with their effect.

9 Attach the strip of checkerboard
self-adhesive shelf paper to the
section of the mailbox's sides and
top where they meet its back end,
starting at the bottom edge of one
side and wrapping it over and around
the top so that it ends at the other
side's bottom edge. Burnish the
paper using an old credit card or a
rubber spatula.

Postal Motifs Collage

CHAPTER 4 Fun Curbside Options

WITH just a handful of clip art images, a page or two from an old road atlas stashed in your glove compartment, and a few used mailing labels saved or gathered from friends or neighbors, it's a snap to make this eye-catching mailbox. Its toned-down funky appeal will lend lively punctuation to any driveway or path.

☞ Materials

A variety of black-and-white clip-art symbols with postal themes*

An old map, or pages from a road atlas

A variety of postal receipts and labels

1 clear self-sticking vinyl sheet, 18 x 24 inches (45 x 60 cm)

Black metal mailbox with smooth or finely corrugated surface

(***Note:** You can find copyright-free clip art images with postal themes in books at craft- and art-supply stores, and on a variety of web sites on the Internet.)*

☞ Tool

Sharp craft scissors or a craft knife with fine blade

☞ Instructions

1 Gather black-and-white clip art images with postal themes and enlarge them by photocopying to sizes approximately 2 to 3 inches (5 to 7.5 cm) long x 1½ to 3 inches (3.75 x 7.5 cm) wide. (The shapes of different motifs will determine their enlarged measurements.) Use sharp scissors or a craft knife to cut out the motifs, making sure to leave white space around black images so that the motifs don't "disappear" when attached to the black mailbox. While you have your cutting tool out, cut from your map or atlas pages triangles of all types (equilateral, isosceles, right-angled, etc.) in different sizes. On a table or other work surface, arrange the clip art and triangle cutouts and the postal receipts and packaging labels you've collected into a collage design that pleases you. Have fun experimenting with different compositions, placing some images individually and some in groups or overlapping. Be sure to leave plenty of empty spaces.

2 Peel the backing off the self-sticking vinyl sheet and lay it sticky side up on your work surface. When attached to the box, the 18-inch (45 cm) edge will be aligned with the bottom edges of the box, and the 24-inch (60 cm) side will cover the box from the bottom edge of one side over the top and to the bottom edge of the other side, overlapping by about 2 inches (5 cm)

onto the bottom of the box on each side. Bearing this in mind, transfer your collage design, placing the images face down, onto the vinyl sheet. (**Note:** *Leave a 2-inch [5 cm] border of empty space at each of the 18-inch [45 cm] ends of the vinyl sheet, so that the images in your collage don't wind up on the bottom of the box when the sheet is attached.)*

3 When the collage is complete, turn the mailbox on its side, then carefully lift the vinyl sheet with the attached collage and position one 18-inch (45 cm) side on the bottom of the box about an inch from the edge; press it in place.

4 Next, carefully press the vinyl sheet into place around the underside of the box where it meets the side; use your fingers to smooth out any small bubbles or wrinkles as you go (a few little ones won't detract from the final effect).

Continue to press and smooth the vinyl sheet with collage into place over the side, around the top, and onto the other side of the mailbox, attaching it around the contours of the box where its other side meets the bottom as you did earlier in this step.

5 When the vinyl sheet with collage is in place, press once again around the edges of paper cutouts and along the points where the vinyl ends on the bottom of the box to secure them. Allow the finished collage to adhere to the box overnight before using it.

Mail Carrier Moments

If you've ever doubted rumors that Spot or Rover really does have a particular penchant for besieging mail carriers, Tony Hibrar's tale is sure to confirm them. "A dog once jumped a fence, bit me in the rear, and jumped back over!," says Hribar, who has suffered no less than three dog bites along his Brighton, Michigan, route since he began his career with the U.S. Post Office Department in 1967. Canine encounters are not Hribar's only experience with the animal kingdom during work hours. He has also discovered, among various letters and packages waiting for him inside the mailboxes on his route, a menagerie of frogs, lizards, toads, and fake snakes—mostly left there as pranks by neighborhood children. But Hribar doesn't hold a grudge. In fact, he says, despite their practical jokes (or maybe because of them), chatting and joking with the kids along his route are his favorite parts of the job. They know him by his first name, and occasionally even leave him candy for a treat.

Moonlit Blossoms

DESIGNER
**LAUREY-
FAYE
LONG**

CHAPTER
4
Fun Curbside
Options

THIS mailbox's quietly metallic glow and swirling design of flowers, stars, and abstract flourishes make it a delightful point of interest for rural, neighborhood, or urban scapes. The best part is it's deceptively simple to create—you need not be an accomplished artist to achieve a finished, professional look.

☞ Materials

White metal post-mount mailbox with smooth surface

1 large tube of silicone caulk

Scrap cardboard or heavy paper

Acrylic spray paint in white, black and gold

☞ Tools

Pencil

Assorted tools for manipulating caulk: a comb, fork, cotton swab, small flat brush, and any other items you want to experiment with

☞ Instructions

1 Assemble the mailbox according to the manufacturer's instructions. Note where the flag, when it is raised into the upright position, comes into closest contact with the side of the mailbox. Mark this area lightly with the pencil. (You'll want to avoid applying caulk to this area while you are decorating the mailbox.) Remove the flag.

2 Open the caulk and practice making a variety of shapes and lines on the cardboard or heavy paper. (*Note: You'll find that keeping the tube's tip in contact with the surface produces heavy lines, while holding the tip above the surface and letting the caulk flow through the air produces thin, "swoopy" lines that are less controllable but which can create wonderful effects. While it is still wet, the caulk can be pushed into place with the flat brush. You can also create a wide variety of textures and appearances in the caulk by using combs, forks, and other tools to shape it. If you have disposable gloves, try finger-painting with the wet caulk. Notice that the caulk begins to set within one or two minutes, so any shaping or texturing on the actual mailbox will have to be done immediately.*)

3 If you desire, sketch a design lightly on the mailbox and then use the caulk to trace over it, or you can simply begin applying the caulk freehand (you can also use stencils, although this will dramatically reduce the pleasingly "loose" feel of the design). Cover the front, back, and top, as well as the sides (more is better for this technique!). You can try leaves and flowers, swirls, wavy lines, stars, or other shapes, symbols, and motifs that appeal to you. Overlapping lines and designs can add a lot as well.

4 When you're satisfied with the design, allow the caulk to dry for 12 hours. Then use the white spray paint to lightly paint the caulk so it will match the color of the mailbox.

5 Now you're ready to apply the black and gold paint, to give the box surface its metallic look. It's a good idea to elevate the mailbox on a cardboard box or footstool to prevent paint pooling up around the base of the box. Starting with black paint, very lightly spray paint the box from a distance of 2 or 3 feet (60 or 90 cm), holding the can at an angle to the mailbox's surface. You want the paint to fall on only one side of the raised caulk design, so stand towards the back of the surface you're painting and spray forward. Continually move the can to work your way around the box until you've covered the sides as well as the top, back, and front.

6 Repeat this step with the gold paint, only change the angle of your painting so that the paint falls on the other side of the caulk designs (if you sprayed back-to-front before, then spray front-to-back now). Allow the paint to dry completely before handling the mailbox.

7 Reattach the flag and mount your mailbox.

PECULIAR-LOOKING "CATCHER" ARMS operated by the Railway Post Office allowed clerks to avoid time-consuming stops along routes by grabbing up mail-bags positioned and ready at the station while the train sped along the tracks toward its next destination.

COURTESY OF THE U.S. POSTAL SERVICE

THIS mailbox, with its deep blues and greens and easy-to-paint alpine backdrop, livens up the approach to any home. Whether you choose to decorate your mailbox with a simple mountain vista or add a more ambitious cottage garden scene, you'll have a good-looking mailbox whose look has staying power.

☞ Materials

Black metal post-mount mailbox

Household scouring powder

A couple of old rags or cloths

Oil enamel paint in red, yellow, blue, dark green, black, and white

Paint thinner

☞ Tools

Paintbrushes in assorted sizes

Painter's palette (or piece of cardboard on which to mix colors)

☞ Instructions

1 To prepare the mailbox for painting, wet the exterior surface of the box and liberally sprinkle the household scouring powder on it. Wet one of the rags and work the scouring powder and water into a paste, smearing the paste all over the mailbox. Let the paste sit for a few minutes, then wash it off thoroughly. Allow the mailbox to sit until it is completely dry.

2 Now you're ready to start painting the side of the box without the flag with the simple mountain vista. Begin by mixing a small amount of the blue paint with a large amount of white on your palette. Use a medium-sized paintbrush to apply the paint, starting about 7½ inches (18.8 cm) up from the bottom of the box to the approximate center line of the top of the box. Be sure to clean painbrushes thoroughly with paint thinner between colors and after final use.

3 Next, to create the clouds in the sky, dip a smaller brush in white paint and "stipple" areas over the clouds by holding your brush perpendicular to the surface of the box and dabbing lightly at, rather than brushing, the surface.

4 Add a little red to another batch of the sky-blue formula you mixed in step 2 to create the background mountains. With a medium-sized brush, paint a couple of simple, gently rounded mountain or hill shapes, with one overlapping the other, at the left-hand side of the mailbox where the painted sky ends. The mountain shapes should be approximately 2½ inches (6.3 cm) tall at their peaks; the farthest point of the front mountain shape overlapping the back one should reach about 6½ inches (16.3 cm) from the end of the mailbox across the side. These measurements, and any in ensuing steps, need not be rigidly adhered to—they're just offered to help guide your sense of proportion.

5 Use blue paint (straight, not mixed with any other colors) to add the foreground mountains that extend all the way across the side of the box. With a medium-sized paintbrush, begin to create the foreground mountains' outline about 4½ inches (11.3 cm) from the bottom of the box, just below the mountains you painted in step 4. Slowly brush an upward stroke (allowing most of the previously painted mountains to show) that rises to a small peak next to the front mountain shape you painted in step 4. From there, create a shallow dip and another small peak, then another dip and a gentle upward slope that ends at the other end of the box, as shown in the photograph. Starting about 2½ inches (6.3 cm) from the bottom of the box, fill in the foreground mountain area all the way across the side of the box with blue paint. Then, using the technique described in step 3, generously stipple the foreground

mountains with green paint. Work quickly; if the blue paint dries before you stipple with green, the effect will not be as pleasing.

6 To paint the trees in the forefront of the design, start by using the dark green paint (unmixed) to brush on a tree line that echoes the contours of the foreground mountains you painted in step 5. (The tree line doesn't need to echo the mountains exactly; some variation will make it look more natural.) Fill in the area between the tree line and the bottom of the box.

7 Next, dip an extra small paintbrush in brown paint and paint seven or eight thin tree trunks in the dark green area. Tree trunks can be easily painted by making a simple

Y shape, then adding a thin line or two for extra branches on some of the Y shapes.

8 Mixing dark green paint with different amounts of white, create a few different shades of medium and light green on your palette. Using the different shades, stipple the ends of the tree branches, and around the trees and tree line, to create the look of leaves. Last, use a little yellow paint to lightly stipple the treetops, to give the effect of sunlight dappling the leaves.

9 Repeat steps 2 through 8 on the other side of the mailbox.

10 Let the paint dry thoroughly, then attach the flag to the mailbox and mount.

Woodburned Van Gogh

Woodburned Van Gogh

THIS handsome cedar mailbox gives off wonderful smells as you're woodburning the design. Inspired by Van Gogh's *Wheatfield with Crows*, the landscape design is manageable by beginners (especially with a pattern, provided in figure 1 on page 117) and looks great just about anywhere.

☛ Materials

Landscape pattern
    (see figure 1 on page 117)

Slatted cedar mailbox

Medium-grain sandpaper

Masking tape

Graphite paper

☛ Tools

Sharp pencil

Woodburner with large, rounded
    point and shading point

Ceramic plate, or other burn-
    resistant surface

Needle-nose pliers (optional)

☛ Instructions

1 Using white paper, enlarge the pattern by photocopying to a size that comfortably spans one side of your mailbox.

2 Place the mailbox on a table at a comfortable height for working. Sand the mailbox's surface with the sandpaper until the surface feels smooth. Blow away the dust.

3 Position the pattern on the side of the mailbox you've chosen to decorate, and tape it in place at the top with masking tape. Slide graphite paper underneath with the graphite side against the mailbox surface.

4 Trace the design with a sharp pencil. Move the graphite paper around to reach various parts of the design as you trace.

5 Remove the pattern and graphite paper. Check the lines of the design—fill in any unclear points or broken sections of lines with pencil.

6 Place the woodburner in its holder on the edge of the table. (**Note:** *To protect your work surface, place the woodburner on a ceramic plate or other burn-resistant surface.*) Screw the large, rounded point into the end of the woodburner. Plug it in and wait for it to heat up.

7 Turn the mailbox over, and try the tip out on the bottom edge of the mailbox to see if it is hot enough to burn your design. Get a feel for how quickly you'll need to move the point across the surface of the wood in order to make a line. (**Note:** *Don't press into the wood. There is no relationship between the pressure that you use and the line that you create. Be aware that the longer you allow the point to stay in one place on the wood, the darker it will burn.*)

8 Burn the outlines of the design with the large, rounded point. Move the point across the wood slowly and evenly. As you move the point across the wood, you'll come across knots and bumps. When you hit these areas, you may have to compensate by dragging the point more slowly, or by retracing the design.

9 After outlining the main lines of the design, begin filling in various areas with short, energetic lines that echo the main borders of the design you've established. (These lines don't have to be perfect, nor do they have to be exactly like those shown here.)

10 After you've finished drawing all of the lines that you want, unplug the woodburner and allow the point to cool. Unscrew the point with needle-nose pliers or your fingers. Screw in the shading point.

11 Plug in the woodburner again, and reheat it with the new point. Add "trees" to your design in any areas that you choose by pressing the shading point onto the wood, allowing it to sit for a few seconds (you'll get a nice puff of smoke from this!), and then lifting it. Repeat this motif to fill in areas of forest. Don't make neat rows of trees—try overlapping them, making some darker than others, and moving the point around on the surface in circles to add dark expanses.

12 Continue to use the shading point to burn dark, shadowy areas of your design. (To do this, place the point on the surface and drag it slowly across the section you're working on.)

13 After you've finished burning the mailbox, dust it off to remove flakes of carbon. Add your name to the other side of the box by using the large, rounded point, if you choose.

14 Attach the hardware and the flag, and mount your mailbox.

Mail Note...

Moving the Mail

As long as the mail gets to us when we're expecting it (more or less, at least), we don't worry so much about its mode of transport. Sending and receiving mail is such an everyday routine, we don't give much thought to the complex technology and human endeavor that goes into regular mail service. Until the modern age, mailing a letter was a luxury available only to the wealthy or elite. Here are some ways early societies moved their mail:

• Sometime around 500 B.C., the Persian emperor Cyrus developed the ancient world's longest postal route so that royal commands—sent in the form of clay tablets carried in clay vessels, or "envelopes"—could be carried between what are now Turkey and Iran. The mail was carried by riders on horseback who passed on the mail relay-style to cross 340 miles, including treacherous desert areas.

• For more than a thousand years, the Incas and Mayas of pre-Columbian America used a postal system that used messengers on foot working in a relay system to move correspondence between designated "post houses."

• While many earlier civilizations used horseback or pedestrian postal delivery systems, some eighth-century-A.D. Arab cultures got a head start on air mail, using carrier pigeons to deliver personal and business correspondence.

• Only royalty and the very rich could afford to use early Europe's postal services, and working as a mail carrier in some of these could be treacherous, not to say deadly. Under the reign of Louis II in France, for example, a carrier who delivered the mail late—regardless of the weather or other reasons he might not have been able to be timely—faced harsh punishment or death.

🖝 Materials

Taj Mahal facade pattern
(see figure 1 on page 121)

Flag stem and star pattern
(see figure 2 on page 121)

Poster board

Lumber (see "Cut List")

Exterior primer

20 1½-inch (3.8 cm) galvanized
Phillips-head self-countersink-
ing deck screws

Wood filler

1 1-inch (2.5 cm) wooden knob

Exterior paint in dark red, bright
blue, metallic gold, and black

2 1-inch (2.5 cm) hinges, with
screws

1 2-inch (5 cm) bolt with washers and ¼-inch (6 mm) nut

🖝 Tools

Craft knife

Craft glue

Masking tape

Pencil

Electric drill with Phillips-head
driver bit

¹⁄₁₆-inch (1.5 mm) drill bit

Jigsaw or scroll saw

Sandpaper

Ruler

An assortment of paintbrushes
(small, medium, large)

Screwdriver

HAVE your mail arrive in style with this grand
palace of a mailbox. A simple box and a clev-
erly patterned cutout combine to create the ultimate
abode for your incoming epistles, whether you
correspond with maharajahs or your mother-in-law.

🖝 Cut List

DESCRIPTION	QTY	MATERIAL	DIMENSIONS
Sides, top, and bottom	4	¾-inch (1.9 cm) exterior plywood	6 x 12 inches (15 x 30 cm)
Back	1	¾-inch (1.9 cm) exterior plywood	4½ x 6 inches (11.3 x 15 cm)
Front	1	¾-inch (1.9 cm) exterior plywood	18 x 18 inches (45 x 45 cm)
Flag stem with star	1	¾-inch (1.9 cm) exterior plywood	5 x 16 inches (12.5 x 40 cm)

🖝 Instructions

1 Use a copier to enlarge the facade and flag stem patterns on page 121 to fit your mailbox. Glue the patterns onto the piece of poster board and cut them out with the craft knife. Be sure to cut out all out the arched spaces for windows and the door in the facade pattern.

2 Lay the cutout facade and flag-stem patterns on the front and flag stem plywood pieces and tape them in place with masking tape.

With a pencil, trace the shapes onto the plywood. Remove the patterns and tape.

3 Use the drill and the ¹⁄₁₆-inch (1.5 mm) drill bit to drill a small pilot hole for the saw blade in one corner of each window opening and the door opening of the facade.

4 Use the jigsaw or scroll saw to cut out the Taj Mahal facade from the plywood. Cut out the door

shape very carefully; you will use this piece for the mailbox door. Discard the arch-shaped pieces of plywood cut from the windows. Next, cut out the flag stem and star. With the sandpaper, sand the front of the facade and the interior surfaces of its windows and door; the front of the door piece; and the front of the flag stem and star.

5 Paint the facade, door piece, flag stem with star, and the pieces of plywood for the box itself with a coat of primer. Let the primer dry until it is completely dry to the touch.

6 On both sides of the dome's bottom section where it forms a right angle with the facade's flat top edge, use the ruler to measure up 1 inch (2.5 cm) and mark these points with a pencil. Position the ruler so that it lies straight between these two points, and draw a line between them. On both sides of the facade's front, measure in 2 inches (5 cm) at the top and bottom and again use the ruler to mark a straight line between each set of points.

7 With the screwdriver, assemble the box using the deck screws. Align the outer edges to the side and back pieces so they are flush with the outer edge of the back piece. Attach them to the bottom piece using seven deck screws. Insert three screws through the outer face of the bottom piece into

the edges of each side piece, placing one screw at each corner and one in the middle of each edge. Insert a final screw in the center of the edge of the back piece. Repeat this pattern to attach the top piece to the box. Install another screw through each side about halfway between the top and bottom to attach the back piece of the mailbox. Last, using deck screws, attach the facade to the open end of the assembled box by countersinking two screws through the facade on each side of the door opening, at 2 and 4 inches (5 and 10 cm) from the facade's bottom and approximately ½ inch (1.3 cm) away from the door opening. Fill in around the screw holes with wood fill. Let it dry, then sand it smooth.

8 Use the drill and Phillips-head bit to attach the knob to the door with a deck screw.

9 Drill a ¼-inch (6 mm) hole in the base of the wand, and an identical hole in the box approximately 2 inches (5 cm) from the top and 1 inch (2.5 cm) from the front on the right-hand side.

10 Following the photograph and using the guidelines you created in step 5, paint the dome metallic gold; the outside portions of the facade's front and the door piece blue; and the main section of the facade's front red. Paint the star on the flag stem yellow, and the flag stem blue. Paint the box shape behind the facade gray. Use an extra-small paintbrush to paint each of the seven cutout spires black. Allow all of the areas you have painted to dry thoroughly, then add the finishing touches by painting a small black spire on each side of the dome's bottom where the gold paint meets red, and painting

the surface of the doorknob black. When these have dried, dip the extra-small brush in white paint and make a small dot in the diamond section of each spire. (You can create a little design on the larger spire that tops the dome, as this designer did, if you choose.) Let the painted box dry overnight.

11 Using the hinge screws, attach the door to the front facade with hinges positioned so that their bottom sides are approximately 1¾ and 3½ inches (4.4 and 8.8 cm) up from the bottom of facade on the left-hand side of the door.

12 Bolt the flag stem with star to the box and mount your mailbox.

WHAT THEY WORE

Want to know how many miles it took an official Canadian letter carrier to complete his rounds at the turn of the 19th century? Just count the pairs of moccasins in his closet! In addition to a standard issue navy blue military-style coat and a brass badge emblazoned with the initials "CPO" (Canada Post Office), each carrier was supplied with 40 pairs of moccasins to shield his dedicated soles from wind, rain, and snow. CPO letter carriers also received a winter coat, a fur hat, a raincoat, and 12 lamps to aid them in their deliveries.

Laughing Giraffe

THIS fun, lighthearted design is a wonderful choice for families with small children or daycare centers in need of a kid-pleasing mailbox. But anyone can enjoy its sunny color and charisma.

"Carrier of news and knowledge
Instrument of trade and industry
Promoter of mutual acquaintance
Of peace and good will
Among men and nations

"Messenger of sympathy and love
Servant of parted friends
Consoler of the lonely
Bond of the scattered family
Enlarger of the common life"

—Charles Eliot, *"The Letter"*

(Inscribed on the Smithsonian Institution's National Postal Museum, formerly a Washington, D.C., post office)

☛ Materials

2 sheets of poster board, 22 x 28 inches or larger (55 x 70 cm)

2 sheets of ¾-inch (1.9 cm) exterior plywood, 4 x 8 feet (1.2 x 2.4 m)

Primer

Exterior enamel or latex paint in yellow, orange, black, light blue, purple, aqua, and red

Clear acrylic spray sealer

White metal post-mount mailbox with smooth surface

Mailbox post kit with 40-inch-tall (1 m) post (or build your own from a 4 x 4; see "Mounting and Installing Your Mailbox," pages 11-12)

Galvanized wood screws

☛ Tools

Pencil

Scissors

Masking tape

Jigsaw

Medium sandpaper

Paintbrushes (large, medium, small)

Drill

☛ Instructions

1 Using the photo and the size of your mailbox post as guides, draw an outline of the giraffe onto the poster board. (Depending on the size of your poster board, you may need to use two sheets to accomodate the height of the giraffe.) Cut out the giraffe pattern.

2 Lay one of the sheets of plywood down on a work surface. Center the giraffe pattern on the plywood. Temporarily secure the pattern to the plywood with masking tape. Use a pencil to trace around the pattern, transferring it onto the plywood. Remove the masking tape and pattern, and use a pencil to add facial features and markings to the plywood giraffe.

3 Repeat step 2 using the second piece of plywood.

4 With the jigsaw, cut out the giraffe shapes from both pieces of plywood.

5 Sand all the edges of both giraffe shapes, then apply a coat of primer to the sanded edges, the front, and the back of the plywood shapes. Allow the primer to dry, then sand the edges again and apply a second coat of primer over all the plywood shapes.

6 Now you are ready to paint the plywood shapes. Using the small and medium paintbrushes, apply a coat of black paint to the edges and back sides of both shapes. Allow the paint to dry thoroughly.

7 With a large brush, paint the front sides of both plywood giraffes yellow. Let them dry until the paint is dry to the touch.

8 Following the photograph, use small and medium paintbrushes to outline the overall shapes and define the faces of both giraffes with black paint. (These outlines should be ¼ to ½ inch [6 mm to 1.25 cm] at any given point.) Do not yet outline the sides of the giraffes where the curved manes are located.

9 Next, you can create the giraffes' manes, spots, and tufts. To make the manes, begin at the point where each giraffe's ear, jaw, and neck meet, and paint a black outline approximately 1¼ inches (3.1 cm) wide down the length of the neck to the bottom. Now paint the spots that extend from the manes. Starting about 3¼ inches (8.1 cm) down from the points at which you began the mane outlines, paint rounded rectangle shapes 4 inches (10 cm) long and extending 2¼ inches (5.6 cm) from the interior mane outlines. Measure 2 inches (5 cm) down along the outlines and make second spots the same size as the first ones; the last two spots should be slightly bigger, about 5½ x 3¼ inches (13.8 x 8.1 cm) each

and spaced 2 inches (5 cm) away from the other spots and one another. Paint three overlapping small black tufts, about 2¼ inches (5.6 cm) tall, with rounded bottoms and pointed tops, between each giraffe's ear and knobbed horn. (One tuft will overlap the horn with no knob on top.)

10 On both giraffes, use a small brush and black paint to finish the facial features by painting the eyes and eyebrows, nostrils, and mouth.

11 With small and medium brushes, finish painting the giraffes by using orange paint to cre-ate shadows and light blue paint to add highlights, following the photograph. Set both painted giraffes aside to dry overnight. When they are thoroughly dry, apply one to two coats of acrylic sealer to both giraffes, allowing each coat to dry before applying the next.

12 Paint the mailbox purple and let the paint dry completely. Following the photo, paint variously sized, simple aqua leaves and red flowers onto the box in a pleasing arrangement. Allow the painted box to dry completely.

13 When both the giraffes and the mailbox are dry, you're ready to assemble your post and mount the mailbox according to the manufacturer's instructions. Next, appropriately position one of the painted plywood giraffes against the post. With a drill, bore two holes through the giraffe and into the post—one about 9 1/2 inches (23.8 cm) down from the top of the giraffe's head, and the other about 15 inches (37.5 cm) up from the bottom of the neck. Install a galvanized screw through each hole to secure the plywood to the post. Repeat this process with the remaining plywood giraffe on the other side of the post, making sure the giraffes are aligned. If you choose, paint the screw heads to blend in with the giraffe's color. Your mailbox is ready to go in the ground.

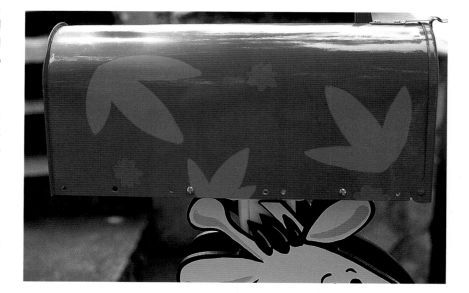

Balancing Act

DESIGNER
NORRIS HALL

CHAPTER 5
Creative Carpentry

WHAT'S not to love about this bright and happy seal balancing a polka-dotted mailbox "ball" on the end of its nose? A great bet if you have children or are still a kid at heart, this whimsical design is also a delightful option if you need a mailbox for a seaside summerhouse.

☛ Materials

2 sheets of ¾-inch (1.9 cm) exterior plywood, 4 x 8 feet (1.2 x 2.4 m)

2 sheets of poster board, 22 x 28 inches (55 x 70 cm) or larger

Primer

Exterior enamel or latex paint in purple, light purple, blue, black, yellow, and orange

Clear acrylic sealer

White metal post-mount mailbox with smooth surface

Mailbox post kit with 40-inch-tall (1 m) post (or build your own from a 4 x 4; see "Mounting and Installing Your Mailbox," pages 11–12)

4 Galvanized wood screws

☛ Tools

Masking tape

Pencil

Jigsaw

Medium sandpaper

Paintbrushes (large, medium, small)

Drill

Screwdriver

☛ Instructions

1 Using the photo and the size of your mailbox post as guides, draw an outline of the seal onto the poster board. (Depending on the size of your poster board, you may need to use two sheets to accomodate the height of the seal.) Cut out the seal pattern.

2 Lay one of the sheets of plywood down on a work surface. Center the giraffe pattern on the plywood. Temporarily secure the pattern to the plywood with masking tape. Use a pencil to trace around the pattern, transferring it onto the plywood. Remove the masking tape and pattern, and use a pencil to add facial features and markings to the plywood seal.

3 Repeat step 2 using the second piece of plywood.

4 With the jigsaw, cut out the seal shapes from both pieces of plywood.

5 Sand all the edges of both seal shapes, then apply a coat of primer to the sanded edges, the front, and the back of the plywood shapes. Allow the primer to dry, then sand the edges again and apply a second coat of primer over all the plywood shapes.

6 Now you are ready to paint the plywood shapes. Using the small and medium paintbrushes, apply a coat of black paint to the edges and back sides of both shapes. Allow the paint to dry thoroughly.

7 With a medium or large brush, paint the front flippers of both plywood seals blue. Apply the blue paint on the flipper only up to where it meets the seal's body.

8 Next, paint the remaining unpainted surfaces of the front sides of both plywood seals purple. Try to make the area where the seal's blue front flipper and purple body meet as neat as possible. It doesn't have to be perfect, since later you'll be covering the joins with black outlines. Don't move on to the next step until the purple paint is dry to the touch.

9 With the small and medium paintbrushes, paint a long, thin, curving blue shadow just behind the back flipper of each seal, as shown in the photograph. Follow the photograph to paint another blue shadow along the back curves of both seals' tails. Let the blue paint dry before proceeding.

10 The next step is to add definition and detail to the seals' shapes with black outlines and accents. Use a small or medium brush and black paint to outline the overall shapes, and to outline and accent the eyes, mouths, whiskers, noses, fins, and tails, as shown in the photograph. Keep the outlines ¼ to ½ inch (6 mm to 1.25 cm) wide at all points. Wait until the paint is dry to the touch before moving on to the next step.

11 With small and medium paintbrushes, add finishing highlights in light purple and blue as shown in the photo. Set both plywood seals aside to dry overnight. When they have dried completely, apply one to two coats of clear acrylic sealer to each plywood seal, allowing each coat to dry before applying the next.

12 Paint the mailbox yellow, and set it aside until it is dry to the touch; then paint large orange circles on it to give a "beach ball" effect.

13 When both the plywood seals and the mailbox are dry, you're ready to assemble your box. Assemble your post and mount the mailbox according to the manufacturer's instructions. Position one of the plywood seals against the post as desired. With a drill, bore a hole through the plywood at the approximate center of the seal's body and into the post. Secure the plywood shape to the post using two galvanized screws. Repeat this process with the remaining plywood shape, ensuring that the seals are aligned. If you choose, paint the screw heads purple to blend in with the seal's overall body color. Your mailbox is ready to be installed.

Mail Carrier Moments

"Neither snow nor rain nor heat nor gloom of night stays these couriers from the swift completion of their appointed rounds," reads the well-known motto of the postal service. And while carriers like Kathie Grable certainly undergo their share of overcoming the elements and other inconveniences, Grable finds lots of perks on the job, too. One of the addressees on her rural route faithfully chills a bottle of water for her in the freezer each summertime night, placing it in the mailbox for Grable to pick up with the outgoing mail the next day. By the time Grable swings by the house, the summer sun is beating down and the cold water makes for a perfect refreshment. Need more convincing that the job has its rewards? When the flora is in bloom, two young boys who live along Grable's route deposit an enchanting bouquet of wildflowers in their mailbox for her to find every afternoon. No surprise she's been at the job for 14 years!

Dutch Flowerpots

DESIGNER
MIKE DURKIN

CHAPTER **5** Creative Carpentry

A **GREAT** woodworking project for beginners, this planter mailbox, with its decorated slip-on cover, is a wonderful choice if you live in a pastoral setting. Pop in small pots filled with new blooms from your garden, and it can't help but brighten up any day.

☛ Materials

Lumber (see "Cut List" on page 74)

Primer

1¼-inch (3 cm) drywall screws

Wood putty

Wood glue

6d finishing nails

Exterior paints in white, green, pastels, or other desired colors

Floral or other stencils (optional)

White metal post-mount mailbox

Flower pots to fit 3⅝-inch-diameter (9 cm) pockets

Note: *For additional guidance in constructing the Dutch Flowerpots, refer to the helpful exploded-view drawing in figures 1 and 2 on page 122.*

☛ Tools

Jigsaw

Compass (optional)

Pencil

Medium sandpaper

Paintbrushes (large and medium)

Drill, with 1/16-inch (1.5 mm) bit and ¼-inch thick (6 mm) countersink bit

Screwdriver

Hammer

☛ Instructions

1 Using the jigsaw, cut all the pieces of the mailbox planter to the dimensions specified in the "Cut List" on page 74.

2 To shape the curved facade, measure in 2 inches (5 cm) from each upper corner and mark. Then measure 2 inches (5 cm) down from each corner and mark. Use a compass or draw a freehand arc to connect the two points at each corner. To shape the planter shleves, meaxure 1¾ inches (4.4 cm) from each outer corner and mark. Then, use a compass or draw a freehand arc to connect the two points, forming a curve at each outside corner. Cut out the curved facade and planter sheves with the jigsaw. Sand the edges of all the pieces smooth with the medium sandpaper.

☛ Cut List

DESCRIPTION	QTY	MATERIAL	DIMENSIONS
Front facade	1	$1/4$-inch (6 mm) plywood	$7^{7}/8$ x 14 inches (20 x 35 cm)
Frame sides	2	$3/4$-inch (1.9 cm) pine shelving	$8^{1}/8$ x $9^{3}/8$ inches (20.3 x 23.4 cm)
Frame center	1	$3/4$-inch (1.9 cm) pine shelving	$7^{7}/8$ x $8^{1}/8$ inches (19.8 x 20.3 cm)
Side planters	2	$3/4$-inch (1.9 cm) pine shelving	$7^{1}/8$ x $8^{1}/8$ inches (17.8 x 20.3 cm), with rounded exterior corners and centered $3^{1}/2$ inch (8.8 cm) diameter holes

3 With a paintbrush, apply a coat of primer to each section of the mailbox, and set each aside to dry completely.

4 Assemble the side planters first, as shown in figure 1 on page 122. Postion the planter shelf so that the straight edge is flush with the outer face of one side of the center frame. Insert three drywall screws through the back of the center frame's bottom edge to attach the planter shelf. Repeat with the remaining planter shelf on the opposite side of the center frame.

5 To complete the center frame body, position the center frame piece so it rests on the top inside edges of the frame side pieces. Attach the center piece to the sides using three countersunk drywall screws on each side. Insert the screws down through the top of the center piece into the top edges of the side pieces, as shown in figure 2 on page 122. Patch the screw holes with wood putty.

6 At this point, it's a good idea to slip the frame over your mailbox to make sure it fits. Make any necessary adjustments to the frame body now, before attaching the front facade.

7 Apply wood glue to the front edges of the frame center and side pieces, and to the back of the front facade where it will meet the center frame. Allow the wood glue to set for a few minutes, then press the front facade firmly in place on the center frame, lining the bottom edges up with the bottom of the frame. Use the hammer to secure the front facade with the 6d nails, inserting three nails through the front of each side of the facade into the side edges of the frame side pieces.

8 After the mailbox planter has been completely assembled, apply two coats of white (or other desired color) exterior paint to the outside of the structure, allowing the paint to dry thoroughly between coats. After the paint has dried, use stencils or your own designs and other paint colors to decorate the planter. In addition to decorative accents, you may also want to add your name and house number to the planter with paints or self-adhesive lettering—the high "forehead" of the facade provides the perfect place for this. Let all paint dry to the touch before inserting potted plants and fitting the cover onto your mailbox.

9 Once all the paint has dried completely, place the mailbox planter over your mailbox. Fill the planter holes with colorful potted plants, flowering vines, or other items of your choice, and brighten your mail carrier's day!

Secret-Door Hold-All

DESIGNER ROBIN CLARK

NEED an attractive and decidedly clever mailbox with a special gift for holding oversized envelopes? A special swivel-up front door on this design offers easy access for both the letter carrier and yourself—just think: no more shredding your fingers as you attempt to wrest a pile of folded catalogs from a too-tiny mailbox!

> *"Gentlemen do not read each other's mail."*
>
> —Henry L. Stimson, Secretary of State under U.S. President Herbert Hoover

☞ Cut List

Note: all wood is ¾-inch (1.9 cm) thick northern white cedar.

Desc	Qty	Dimensions
Roof	2	3 x 7 inches (7.5 x 17.5 cm)
Back	1	11¾ x 24 inches (29.4 x 60 cm)
Flap	1	6 x 13 inches (15 x 32.5 cm)
Door	1	9¾ x 14 inches (24.4 x 35 cm)
Sides	2	4¾ x 15¾ inches (11.9 x 39.4 cm)
Floor	1	4 x 9¾ inches (10 x 24.4 cm)
Entry	1	4 x 6¾ inches (10 x 16.9 cm)
Toggles	2	¾ x 2 inches (1.9 x 5 cm)

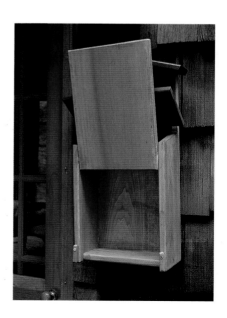

☞ Materials

Lumber (see "Cut List")

Exterior paint in forest green

Early American wood stain

#6 1¾-inch (4.4 cm) coarse thread Phillips-head screws

10-inch (25 cm) brass plate piano hinge with screws

2 1-inch (2.5 cm) nails

6-inch (15 cm) length of sturdy metal chain for wall-mounting

☞ Tools

Table saw, jigsaw, or circular saw

Drill with ⅛-inch (3 mm) and 1¾-inch (4.4 cm) bits

Medium-grade sandpaper

Paintbrushes (small, medium, large)

#2 Phillips-head screwdriver

Hammer

☞ Instructions

1 With a saw, complete cutting of the pieces: Cut the top ends of the back and entry pieces to a 150° peak (15° cut on each side of the center-point at the top). Cut the top end of each side piece to a 15° angle. On the entry piece, mark a point 2¼ inches (5.6 cm) from the peak down a center line and drill a ¾-inch (1.9 cm) hole. (This hole simulates the entry hole of an actual birdhouse.) Make a 15° bevel cut on both ends of one face of each roof piece. Make a 15° bevel cut along the back edge of the flap piece.

2 Using medium sandpaper, a router, or a file, round all edges of the pieces.

3 Paint the top faces do the roof pieces and the bottom face of the flap piece dark green (or the color of your choice). Paint the inside of the birhouse "entry" hole black. Apply one or two coats of wood stain to all unpainted surfaces of the pieces.

4 In the back piece, drill two pilot holes ⅜ inches (9 mm) in from each edge, one 4 inches (10 cm) and one 12 inches (30 cm) from the bottom end. With the tall edge to the back and the bottom ends square, attach the side pieces to the back with screws. (The front height of the sides will be 14 inches [35 cm] and the back height 15¾ inches [39.4 cm].)

5 On each side piece, drill three pilot holes: Place the first pilot hole through the side face ⅜ inch (9 mm) in from the front edge and 1¾ inches (1.9 cm) down from the top slanted end; place the second pilot hole through the side face ⅜ inches (9 mm) up from the bottom end and 2 inches (5 cm) from the front edge; and place the third pilot hole on the front edge, ¾ inches (1.9 cm) up from the bottom.

6 Position the floor piece so it is ⅛ inch (3 mm) up from the bottom ends of the back and sides. Press it tightly to the back and secure it with two screws inserted through the faces of the sides.

7 Place the door piece even with the bottom of the sides and flush to the front edges of the sides, and secure with two screws through the pilot holes in the top of the side faces. To allow the door to open easily, back out and reset the screws several times.

8 Position the entry piece so that its peak matches that of the back and secure it with two screws from the back.

9 On each roof piece, drill two pilot holes ⅜ inches (9 mm) in from the back edge about 2 inches (5 cm) apart. Hold the roof pieces flush with the back so the angled peak where they meet matches snugly, and secure them in place with two screws in each roof half.

10 Position the piano hinge along the beveled back edge of the flap piece so that it overlaps the flap top face and is 1-¾ inches (1.9 cm) from each end. Secure the hinge to the back edge of the flap with the hinge screws. Then, rest the hinged edge of the flap on the tops of the angled sides and secure the hinge to the back with the remaining hinge screws.

11 Drill a pilot hole in each of the two toggles. Center the hole ¾ inch (1.9 cm) from one end.

Position the holes in the toggles over the holes in the front edges of each side. Secure them with screws loosely enough so that they can be turned and tightly enough to hold their positions.

12 To mount the mailbox, hammer two nails halfway into the back, about 3 inches (7.5 cm) in from each side and 3 inches (7.5 cm) down from the top of the roof. Loop the ends of the length of chain over the nails, then hammer each nail flat so the chain is secured.

BEFORE THE ADVENT OF ELECTRIC LIGHTING, post office work areas, such as this scene from 1892, typically included many big windows.

COURTESY OF THE U.S. POSTAL SERVICE

Covered Bridge

DESIGNER
MIKE DURKIN

CHAPTER **5** Creative Carpentry

TRANSPORT your mail carrier to a cheerful version of New England every day with this colorful covered bridge mailbox. Its versatility as a slip-on cover allows you to remove it in the worst of winter weather, saving its sprightly colors for spring's return.

☛ Materials

Lumber (see "Cut List")

Exterior paints in white, dark green, dark red, and bright yellow

Stencils (optional)

6d finishing nails

Wood glue

¾-inch (1.9 cm) brads

1¼-inch (3 cm) drywall screws

Flag kit

White metal post-mount mailbox, 6½ x 8 x 18¾ inches (16.3 x 20 x 46.9 cm)

☛ Tools

Ruler and/or tape measure

Scroll saw or jigsaw

Tin snips to trim aluminum flashing

Pencil

Compass

Medium sandpaper

Paintbrushes (small, large)

Drill with ½-inch (1.3 cm) drill bit and countersink bit for drywall screws

Hammer

☛ Instructions

1 Measure and cut out all the pieces listed in the cut list using the scroll saw or jigsaw and the tin snips. Cut the roof ends to a 35° angle on each side. Next, use the pencil and compass to draw four semi-circular dips along the

☛ Cut List

DESCRIPTION	QTY	MATERIAL	DIMENSIONS
Mailbox sides	2	¾-inch (1.9 cm) pine shelving	11 x 19½ inches (27.5 x 49 cm)
Mailbox back	1	¾-inch (1.9 cm) pine shelving	8½ x 9¼ inches (21.3 x 23.1 cm)
Roof pieces	2	¼-inch (6 mm) plywood	6½ x 16 Inches (16.3 x 40 cm)
Roof cover	1	aluminum flashing	13½ x 16⅛ inches (33.8 x 40.3 cm)
Roof sides	2	¾-inch (1.9 cm) pine shelving	3 x 14 inches (7.5 x 35 cm)
Roof ends	2	¾-inch (1.9 cm) pine shelving	4½ x 8 inches (11.3 x 20 cm)
Bridge floor	1	¾-inch (1.9 cm) pine shelving	6¾ x 19½ inches (16.9 x 48.8 cm)
Pillars	8	½-inch-diameter (1.3 cm) dowel rods	5 inches (12.5 cm)
Flag base	1	¾-inch (1.9 cm) pine shelving	1¾ x 2½ inches (4.4 x 6.3 cm) (or cut to fit your flag kit mount)

top edge of each mailbox side piece. Draw the first dip 3⅜ inches (8.4 cm) back from the front edge. Set the compass so that each dip is 2½ inches (6.3 cm) wide x 1¼ inches (3.1 cm) deep. Space the dips approximately 1¾ inches (4.4 cm) apart. Using the scroll saw, cut out the dips in the tops of each mailbox side piece. Repeat this process along the bottom edge of each roof side piece, making three 2½- x 1¼-inch (6.3 x 3.1 cm) arcs

in each piece. Start the first arc 1½ inches (3.8 cm) in from the front edge of each piece, and space the 2½-inch (6.3 cm) wide arcs approximately 1¾ inches (4.4 cm) apart. Cut out the arcs with the jigsaw or scroll saw. Finally, draw and cut out one arc in the center of each roof end piece. The arc should be 2¾ inches (6.9 cm) in from the sides of each end piece. Sand the edges of all arcs before proceeding.

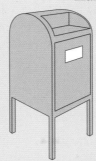

Mail Note...

Global Communications

Mailboxes around the world come in an extraordinary array of colors, shapes, and sizes. Red metal mailboxes dangle from street lamps in Hong Kong. Bright yellow rectangles form the post receptacles in Sweden. Red and yellow boxes hold the mail in Israel (red for intercity and international mail, yellow for local post).

Despite their many incarnations, however, mailboxes the world over sometimes share common symbols. The post horn is one such symbol. The small brazen horn was originally a feature of wartime, when its shrill notes signaled attack or warned of approaching danger. As the years passed, the horn heralded other occasions, from cattle round-ups to the arrival of the mail.

Post horns eventually became standard equipment for mail carriers in many regions of western Europe. Messengers and post-bearers had to learn a number of different horn signals, which allowed them to communicate distress and departure as well as their arrival. Use of the post horn was especially essential in the Swiss Alps; once roads were built that allowed horse-drawn mail coaches to navigate the treacherous mountain passes, postilions blew the horns to signal their presence along the steep winding roads.

Although airplanes and automobiles have taken the place of horse-drawn coaches in most modern mail deliveries, the post horn retains a prominent place in many postal services—right on the mailbox! The small brass horn appears in a variety of stylized forms on Austrian, Belgian, Dutch, German, Mexican, Spanish, Swedish, and Swiss mailboxes.

2 Before assembling the covered bridge mailbox, paint the pieces with exterior paints. Apply two coats of paint for full coverage, allowing the paint to dry completely between each coat and before assembling the mailbox. To imitate the design shown here, apply white paint to both sides of the mailbox side and rear pieces; the roof side and end pieces; and the flag base. Paint the bridge floor, the eight dowel rods, and the top edge of the mailbox rear piece dark green. Paint the roof base pieces dark red. Once these pieces have dried, you may wish to stencil a design on the mailbox sides and the roof side and ends before assembling the mailbox.

3 Using the drill and ½-inch (1.3 cm) drill bit, drill 1-inch-deep (2.5 cm) holes between each arc in the bottom edge of each roof side piece. Repeat the process on the top edge of the mailbox side pieces, drilling 1-inch-deep (2.5 cm) holes between each of the arcs, starting after the first arc. The pillars will go in these holes later.

4 To assemble the mailbox, begin by attaching the roof end pieces to the roof sides with the 6d finishing nails and wood glue. Apply a moderate amount of wood glue to the outside ends of the side pieces at front and back, and apply glue to the backsides of the roof end pieces where they will connect with the side pieces. Hammer two nails into the front surface of each side of each roof end piece, so that the nails enter the outside edges of each side piece. Allow the wood glue to dry completely.

5 Attach the roof base to the lower roof structure with wood glue and the ¾-inch (1.9 cm) brads. First, apply wood glue to the top surfaces of the lower roof structure that the roof base will rest on. Also apply glue to the underside of the roof base pieces, where they will connect with the lower roof structure. Allow the glue to set up for a few minutes before placing the base pieces onto the roof structure. Next, place the aluminum flashing roof cover over the roof base pieces,

making sure it is trimmed to exact size. Then, holding the flashing in place, hammer four brads into the outer edge of each half of the roof; four brads along the long edge on each half; and two brads into the middle of each side of the roof to hold the flashing in place securely.

6 Attach the mailbox side pieces to the bridge floor with the 1¼-inch (3.1 cm) drywall screws. First, apply wood glue to the outer edges of the bridge floor, where it will contact the side pieces. Also apply glue to the inner surfaces of the side pieces, where they will contact the floor. Allow the glue to set up a moment to form a strong bond. Next, position the floor so that its bottom edge is 2½ inches (6.3 cm) below the tops of the side pieces. Using the drill, countersink four, evenly spaced drywall screws through each side piece into the outer edges of the floor.

7 Use 6d finishing nails and wood glue to attach the mailbox back piece to the mailbox sides and bridge floor. Apply a moderate amount of wood glue to the outer edges of the back piece, where it will come into contact with the mailbox structure. Do the same on the side and floor pieces, and allow the glue to set up for several minutes. Press the back piece against the structure and hammer into place, inserting four nails into each side and across the top.

8 To attach the flag to the mailbox, measure down 3 inches (7.5 cm) from the top edge of the side piece on the side of the box from which your mail carrier routinely approaches. Position your flag kit on top of the flag base (which should be mounted vertically, unless this doesn't work with your flag kit) and attach the whole assembly to the mailbox with two 1¼-inch (3.1 cm) drywall screws.

9 To connect the top and bottom portions of the covered bridge, apply a moderate amount of wood glue to the top and bottom surfaces of each of the eight dowel rods. Also insert glue into the drilled holes between the arcs of the mailbox and roof side pieces. After allowing the glue to set up for several minutes, insert a dowel into each hole of the mailbox side pieces. Then, place the roof structure on top, making sure to fit a dowel properly and securely into each hole in the roof side pieces. Let the glue dry completely (preferably 24 hours, or overnight) before handling or mounting the mailbox.

10 To mount the Covered Bridge slip-on mailbox onto your standard mailbox, predrill two holes along the bottom edge of each side of the mailbox slip-on cover and mailbox, and attach the cover to the mailbox with 1¼-inch (3 cm) drywall screws. Countersink the screws, if desired, and paint the screw heads white.

CHAPTER

6

Woodworked
Wonders

DESIGNER
MIKE DURKIN

CHAPTER 6

Woodworked Wonders

Noah's Ark

WITH its well-executed motif taken from one of the oldest tales in the world, this attractive mailbox cover looks good anywhere and is sure to keep the rain off your mail (even in case of flood!). While making it requires a bit more know-how than some of the projects in this book, it's well worth the effort—there won't be a better looking mailbox on the block.

Note: For additional guidance in constructing the Noah's Ark cover, refer to the helpful exploded-view drawings on page 114.

☛ Cut List

DESCRIPTION	QTY	MATERIAL	DIMENSIONS
Ark sides	2	¾-inch (1.9 cm) pine shelving	11 x 25 inches (27.5 x 62.5 cm)
Ark floor	1	¾-inch (1.9 cm) pine shelving	6½ x 25 inches (16.3 x 62.5 cm)
Ark back	1	¾-inch (1.9 cm) pine shelving	5 x 6½ inches (12.5 x 16.3 cm)
Ark end rails	2	¾-inch (1.9 cm) pine shelving	¾ x 6½ inches (1.9 x 16.3 cm)
House ends	2	¾-inch (1.9 cm) pine shelving	5 x 5½ inches (12.5 x 13.4 cm) cut to match diagram dimensions
House sides	2	¾-inch (1.9 cm) pine shelving	3 x 10 inches (7.5 x 25 cm) panels
House roof	2	¼-inch-thick (6 mm) plywood	5 x 14 inches (12.5 x 35 cm)
Mailbox door	1	¼-inch-thick (6 mm) plywood	6¼ x 9 inches (15.6 x 22.5 cm)
Animals		¾-inch (1.9 cm) Scrap pine	(see patterns in figure 3 on page 114)

☛ Materials

Lumber (see "Cut List")

Wood glue

1¼-inch (3 cm) drywall screws

Exterior paints (cream, blue, brown, yellow, orange, grey)

Black and brown fine-tip permanent markers

6d finishing nails

Brown wood stain

Standard post-mount mailbox with recessed bottom, 6 ½ x 8 x 18 ¾ inches (16.3 x 46.9 cm)

8d finishing nails

¾-inch (1.9 cm) long nuts

¼-inch (6 mm) bolts

Carbon paper (optional)

Glue gun and glue sticks (optional)

Mailbox flag kit (optional)

☛ Tools

Scroll saw

Belt sander or coarse sandpaper

Hand drill with ¹⁄₁₆-inch bit and ¼-inch (6 mm) countersink bit

Screwdriver

Paintbrushes

Yardstick

Hammer

Pencil

Compass (optional)

☛ Instructions

1 Use the scroll saw to cut all of the pieces to the correct dimensions as listed in the "Cut List." To shape the ark sides, measure 5½

inches (13.8 cm) down from the top corners of each side piece and mark. Measure 6 inches (15 cm) in from the bottom corners of each side piece and mark. Use a compass or draw a freehand arc to connect the marked points, then cut the curved pieces with the scroll saw. Sand the edges of each piece to a smooth finish using the belt sander or coarse sandpaper.

2 Assemble the ark sides and floor using the wood glue and eight drywall screws—four on each side, countersunk and evenly spaced. Position the ark floor so that it rests approximately ¾ inch (1.9 cm) below the top of the side pieces, then position the ark back piece between and flush with the ends of the side pieces at the back of the ark. Countersink four drywall screws (two on each side) through the outer edges of the side pieces into the edges of the ark back to hold it in place. Glue the end rails in place on top of the ark floor, at each end of the ark, so that they fit snugly between the tops of the side pieces and are flush with the end of the floor piece.

3 Once the ark body has been assembled, use the paintbrush and exterior cream and brown paints to paint it. Apply two coats of cream paint to the outside and inside of the ark, allowing the paint to dry completely between coats. Apply soft strokes of brown paint at random along the sides and edges of the ark to give it a more wooden look. Allow to dry completely.

4 After the paint has dried completely, use the yardstick and the fine-tip permanent brown marker to draw boards on the outside of the ark. Make the boards approximately 1⅛ inches (2.8 cm) wide. You may want to practice a few lines in pencil first to get the hang of it while you can still erase.

5 Assemble the ark house with the wood glue and 6d nails. Position the house end pieces so that they overlap the ends of the side pieces, and hammer four nails into the front of each house end piece (two on each side) to attach them to the side pieces.

6 Once the ark house sides and ends are securely assembled, apply two coats of the blue exterior paint to the outside of the structure, allowing the paint to dry thoroughly between coats. After the blue paint has dried completely, use the dark and light brown paints to create two windows on each side of the house and a barn-like door on each end of the house. Add more detail (such as board slats on the doors) with the fine-point brown permanent marker after the paint has dried, if desired.

7 Use a different paint brush to apply one to two coats of brown wood stain to both sides of each roof piece. Also apply two coats of stain to the mailbox door piece. Allow the stain to dry completely between coats.

8 To attach the roof to the house, use the wood glue, hammer, and 8d finishing nails. Position each roof piece flat against the slanted edges of the house end pieces. You should have an approximate ½-inch (3.8 cm) overhang on each edge of the roof. Run a pencil around the underside of the roof pieces, under the overhangs, to mark where the roof pieces meet the house pieces. Apply wood glue along these lines and to the top edges of the house structure, and allow the glue to sit for a few minutes to become tacky. Then, replace one roof piece, pressing it securely to the house, and hammer two 8d finishing nails through the roof into the top edges of the house end pieces (one nail on each side of the roof). Repeat with the remaining roof piece. The roof pieces will not meet completely at the roof's peak.

9 Remove the latch from the door of your mailbox. Place the wooden mailbox door piece on top of the actual mailbox door, and use the pencil to mark the position of the latch holes on the backside of the door piece. Drill ¾-inch-wide (1.9 cm) holes at these points. Reposition the door latch on the outside of the wooden door piece, and attach the door piece to the mailbox door with the two ¾-inch-long (1.9 cm) nuts and ¼-inch (6 mm) bolts. Be sure the door will open and close easily. If it seems sticky or hard to move, use the saw to shave the edges of the wooden door piece so that it slides easily inside the ark body.

10 With a pencil and using the animal patterns in figure 3 on page 114 as a guide, recreate the animal shapes on the scrap pine board. Make slight variations to the elephant and giraffe patterns to create the raised-trunk and bent-neck versions, if desired. If you're not comfortable drawing freehand, place a piece of carbon paper between the templates and the wood and transfer the patterns onto the pine surface. Cut out each animal shape with the scroll saw. Apply two coats of exterior paint to each animal to provide protection from the weather. Use a mix of light and dark brown paint for the camels; grey for the elephants; and a base color of bright yellow followed by bright orange spots for the giraffes. Be sure to allow the paint to dry completely between coats. Use the fine-tip permanent black and brown markers to apply detail to the animals, such as eyes, mouths, ears, wrinkles, and other markings. Attach the animals to the deck of the ark with wood glue or a hot glue gun after the mailbox has been completely assembled. For a more sturdy attachment, fasten each animal in place with wood screws

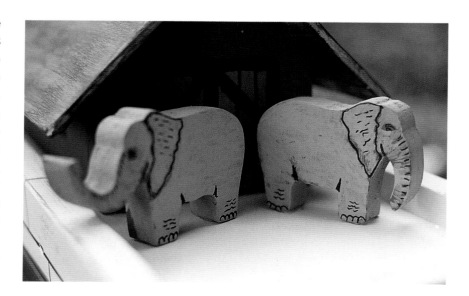

inserted from beneath the ark floor before attaching the mailbox cover to the actual mailbox.

11 Attach the flag that came with the mailbox to the outside of the ark with drywall screws, or purchase a separate flag kit and attach according to the manufacturer's instructions. Be sure to position the flag on the right side of the mailbox, and place it 1 inch (2.5cm) below the top edge of the ark side. The flag must be able to move freely up and down (make sure the ark roof does not get in the way).

12 To attach the Noah's ark mailbox cover to your mailbox, place the ark over the mailbox so that the end of the mailbox is flush with the back piece of the ark (you should have approximately a 3-inch [7.5cm] ledge on the top and sides of the ark at the front of the mailbox). Look for predrilled holes along the bottom lip of your mailbox. If there are no existing holes, drill one hole on each side to accommodate 1¼-inch (3cm) drywall screws. Last, insert one 1¼-inch (3cm) drywall screw into each side of the ark from the inside of the mailbox bottom, and your ark is ready to sail!

WHY RED?

Why are Canadian mailboxes red? The rosy hue of Canada's post and parcel boxes recalls the early influence of the British Empire. As the conventional color of British mailboxes, red easily became the standard color for mailboxes in Canada. In addition to following in British footsteps, the favored postal color represents one half of the country's national colors, red and white, which King George V chose for Canada's coat of arms in 1921. The Canadian coat of arms and the color red remain a fixture of the country's mailboxes today.

Medieval Castle

DESIGNER
MIKE DURKIN

Medieval Castle

ADD a royal touch to your surroundings with this wonderful medieval-castle-style mailbox cover. Fitted over a plain mailbox from the hardware store or home improvement center, it transforms the ordinary into the extraordinary with a stately statement that will wow neighbors and passersby, and turn your daily down-the-driveway-to-the-mailbox routine into an enchanting experience.

Note: *For additional guidance in constructing the Medieval Castle, refer to the helpful exploded-view drawings on page 119.*

☛ Materials

Lumber (see "Cut List")

White metal post-mount mailbox, 6½ x 8 x 18¾ inches (16.3 x 20 x 46.9 cm)

Primer

Exterior enamel or latex paints in gray, brown, blue, and red

1¼-inch (3 cm) drywall screws

Wood putty

Wood glue

Fine-tip permanent black marker

Wood screws (small)

Glue gun and glue sticks (optional)

4 small tacks (for inner braces)

2 small nuts

2 small bolts

Small metal chain, 8 to 10 inches (20 to 25 cm) long

4 screw eyes

☛ Tools

Scroll saw

Hand saw

Tin snips

An assortment of paintbrushes

Drill with screwdriver bit, countersink bit, regular bit

Screwdriver

Yardstick

Hammer

> *"The Post Office Department is like a great root spreading many feet under ground and nourishing the mighty oak. It is the tap root of civilization."*
>
> —U.S. Representative Joseph G. Cannon, 1927, from *Uncle Joe Cannon* by L. White Busby

☛ Cut List

DESCRIPTION	QTY	MATERIALS	DIMENSIONS
Castle sides	2	¾-inch (1.9 cm) pine shelving	11 x 19½ inches (27.5 x 48.8 cm) with notches
Castle back	1	¾-inch (1.9 cm) pine shelving	11 x 12½ inches (27.5 x 31.3 cm)
Castle front	1	¾-inch (1.9 cm) pine shelving	11 x 12½ inches (27.5 x 31.3 cm), door cutout 6½ x 9 inches (16.3 x 22.5 cm)
Castle door	1	¾-inch (1.9 cm) plywood	6⅛ x 8½ inches (15.3 x 21.3 cm)
Castle door stone blocks	15	¾-inch (1.9 cm) pine shelving	1⅜ x 1⅜ inches (3 x 3 cm)
Castle roof	1	¾-inch (1.9 cm) pine shelving	11 x 19¹¹⁄₁₆ inches (27.5 x 49.2 cm)
Castle towers	4	1½-inch-diameter (3.8 cm) PVC piping	13 inches (32.5 cm)
Tower inserts	4	¾-inch (1.9 cm) pine shelving	1½-inch-diameter (3.8 cm) circles
Tower lookout walls	4	¾-inch (1.9 cm) pine shelving	4-inch-diameter (10 cm) circles, cut according to fig. 2 on page 119
Tower lookout wall blocks	20	¾-inch (1.9 cm) pine shelving	½ x 1¼ inches (1.3 x 3 cm)
Inner braces	2	¾-inch (1.9 cm) pine shelving	2⁷⁄₁₆ x 8½ inches (6 x 21.3 cm)
Flagpoles	4	¼-inch (6 mm) dowel rods	6 inches (15 cm)
Flags	4	aluminum pie pans or aluminum flashing	1½ x 4 inches (3.8 x 10 cm)

☛ Instructions

1 Using the scroll saw, cut out the wooden pieces of the castle according to the cut list and the figures on page 119. To make the flagpoles, use a hand saw to cut 1¾-inch-long (4.4 cm) slits in the ends of each 6-inch-long (15 cm) dowel piece. Also at this point, make sure the tower inserts you have cut out fit smoothly and snugly in the ends of the PVC piping (castle towers). If they do not, reshape them as necessary to fit. To make the castle door, trace the door of the actual mailbox onto the plywood and cut out the shape. Using tin snips, cut the aluminum flag pieces into triangles.

2 Apply a coat of primer to all of the wooden castle pieces and allow the primer to dry completely. Using a paintbrush and the exterior paint, apply two coats of gray paint to all of the wooden castle pieces, except the flagpoles (blue) and the castle door (brown). Also paint the PVC pipe pieces gray. Allow the paint to dry completely between coats. Paint the aluminum flags red on both sides and allow them to dry completely.

3 Once the paint has dried completely, assemble the body of the castle. Start by attaching the castle roof to the side pieces. Using the drill and screwdriver bit, or a screwdriver, countersink four drywall screws into the side edge of one

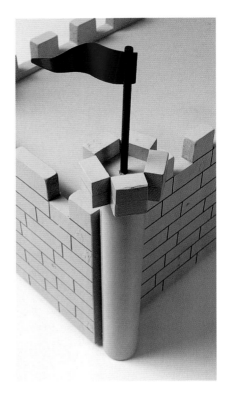

5 To affix the 15 stone blocks to the castle front with the wood glue, start by arranging the stone blocks around the curvature of the door cutout. Stack four blocks vertically on each side of the door, then begin angling the blocks slightly around the curve, and place one block upright at the top center of the curve (this block will rest directly above the door latch). Once you are comfortable with your arrangement, apply a moderate amount of wood glue to the back of each stone and to the castle front. Allow the glue to set up for a few minutes to ensure a strong bond, then press each block securely in place and allow the glue to dry completely.

6 Using the yardstick and the fine-tip permanent black marker, draw "stones" on the outside of the four castle walls. Make each stone approximately 1¼ inches (3 cm) high and 3 inches (7.5 cm) long, and alternate the placement of stones from row to row to give the appearance of stonework.

7 Attach the castle towers to the four corners of the castle body using the drywall screws. Drill two pilot holes into each tower near the top and bottom, then drill two drywall screws through the tower pilot holes from inside the castle body.

8 Drill a ½-inch-deep (1.3 cm) hole in the center of each tower lookout inserts for the flag-poles. Use small wood screws to attach the tower lookout bases to the tower lookout walls. Drill one screw through the bottom of each insert up into the bottom of each wall piece. Affix the tower lookout blocks with wood glue, allowing the glue to set up before attaching the blocks. Place five blocks on each lookout, aligning them with the segment of wall beneath them. Place the lookout tower walls into the towers

9 To attach the flagpoles, apply wood glue or hot glue to the bottom end of each flagpole (the end without the slit) and press it firmly into the hole in the top of the tower lookout wall piece. Make two bends in each of the four red aluminum flags to give them a blowing-in-the-breeze appearance, and insert each flag into a flagpole slit. The flags should fit snugly in the slits without danger of falling out.

10 To stabilize the Medieval Castle cover on the mailbox, insert the two inner braces inside the castle body. Position one brace on the inside of the castle body, about 5½ inches (13.8 cm) from the back of the castle body. Hammer two tacks into the brace from the outside of the castle wall, one near the top and one near the bottom. Repeat with the remaining brace on the opposite side of the castle. The braces should create a snug fit for the mailbox inside the castle body.

side piece, just below the castellations (the notched pieces spanning the top edges of the castle walls) and into the side edge of the castle roof. Repeat this step to attach the remaining side piece. Fill the screw holes with wood putty, smooth the wood putty out, and touch up the paint job.

4 Using the drill and bit, or screwdriver, attach the castle back to the castle body with two countersunk drywall screws on each side, 2 inches (5 cm) from the bottom and 5 inches (12.5 cm) from the top. Insert three countersunk, evenly spaced drywall screws across the top. Repeat this step to attach the castle front. Fill all the screw holes with wood putty, smooth, and touch up the paint job.

11 Attach the castle door to the actual mailbox door using two nuts and bolts through existing holes, or drill your own holes just below the center of the door. To add the chain to the drawbridge door, screw one screw eye into each outside edge of the plywood door where the shape begins to curve. Insert another screw eye into the outside edge of a stone block on each side of the door shape. Attach a length of chain from the door screw eyes to the stone block screw eyes on each side of the door. Be sure to leave enough slack in the chains to allow the door to open and close freely. Note that the chains will be the only part of the slip-on castle mailbox that connects the castle body to the actual mailbox. Since they are easily removable, however, it will be no problem to take the slip-on cover off when desired.

12 Use wood screws to attach the mailbox flag to the outside of the castle wall. Be sure to place the flag on the right side of the box as you face the box from the road, approximately 1 to 2 inches (2.5 to 5 cm) below the top of the castle wall.

MAIL CARRIERS such as this one in the late 19th century were authorized to wear helmets that closely resembled helmets worn by policemen of the era. U.S. Postal Service regulations also mandated that the carriers wear badges while making their rounds.

COURTESY OF THE U.S. POSTAL SERVICE

DESIGNER **MARK STROM**

CHAPTER 6 Woodworked Wonders

Contemporary Cedar

IF you enjoy working with wood and seek a mailbox combining strong, contemporary lines with the timelessness of West Coast softwood, this cedar creation fits your bill. Not only is cedar celebrated for its rot-resistant longevity, the wood's natural finish is so beautiful that you may have trouble getting your house to live up to your mailbox!

☞ Cut List

DESCRIPTION	QTY	MATERIAL	DIMENSIONS
Mailbox posts	2	cedar	2 x 10 x 60 inches (5 x 25 x 150 cm)
Mailbox post center piece	1	cedar	2 x 10 x 34 inches (5 x 25 x 85 cm)
Mailbox arm supports	2	cedar	2 x $5^{1}/_{4}$ x $28^{1}/_{2}$ inches (5 x 13 x 71.3 cm)
Mailbox cover back piece	1	cedar	$^{3}/_{4}$ x $6^{3}/_{4}$ x $9^{1}/_{8}$ inches (1.9 x 16.9 x 22.8 cm)
Mailbox cover sides	2	cedar	$^{3}/_{4}$ x $9^{1}/_{8}$ x 22 inches (1.9 x 22.8 x 55 cm)
Mailbox cover top piece	1	cedar	$^{3}/_{4}$ x 8 x $23^{3}/_{4}$ inches (1.9 x 15 x 46.3 cm)
Insert for under mailbox	1	cedar	$^{3}/_{4}$ x 6 x $18^{1}/_{2}$ inches (1.9 x 1.8 x 44.4 cm)
Side strips	4	cedar	$^{3}/_{4}$ x $1^{3}/_{4}$ x $22^{1}/_{8}$ inches (55.3 x 1.9 x 4.4 cm)

☞ Materials

Exterior walnut stain

Lumber (see "Cut List")

#8 x 1¼-inch (3 cm) Phillips-head galvanized deck screws

#8 x 2-inch (5 cm) Phillips-head galvanized deck screws

1¼-inch (3 cm) galvanized finishing nails

Metal post-mount mailbox, 6½ x 8½ 18¾ inches (16.3 x 21.3 x 46.9 cm)

⅜-inch (9 mm) wood buttons

Clear oil finish

☞ Tools

Paintbrushes (medium, large)

Ruler

Pencil

5-foot (1.5 m) straightedge

Compass

Jigsaw with 10 tooth-per-inch (tpi) blade

Try square

Phillips-head screwdriver

Drill with #8 countersink bit

Hammer

Nail set*

⅛-inch (3 mm) drill bit

Medium-grade sandpaper

*__Note:__ *While the nail set is not a crucial tool for this project, it will enhance the finished piece; by punching your nails down below the surface of the wood, you can prevent discoloring of the wood, and hide shiny metal nail heads from view.*

☞ Instructions

1 Apply at least one coat of exterior walnut stain to the post center piece and the mailbox strips, according to the manufacturer's instructions. Allow the stain to dry completely.

2 At one end of a 2 x 10 x 60-inch (5 x 25 x 150 cm) piece of lumber, measure in 3 inches (7.5 cm) from the edge and mark this point with the pencil. This will be the top of your mailbox post. On the opposite end, measure in from the same edge and make a mark at 6 1/2 inches (16.3 cm). Using the 5-foot straightedge, draw a diagonal line joining the two points.

3 On the end marked at 6 1/2 inches (16.3 cm), measure up from the edge on the thin side of the diagonal line and make a mark at 18 3/4 inches (46.9 cm). Using this mark as a center, use a compass to draw a 4-inch radius that joins the diagonal line to the edge of the board.

4 On the same edge as the radius was drawn, measure in 1 1/2 inches (3.8 cm) from the edge and mark where this point intersects with the radius. Draw a diagonal line from this point to the outside edge at the bottom of the board.

5 At the top of the post (the end with the mark at 3 inches [7.5 cm]), measure down 2 1/8 inches (5.3 cm) on the straight edge and mark. Draw a diagonal line from this point to the 3-inch (7.5 cm) diagonal point.

6 Repeat the process on the second 2 x 10 x 60-inch (5 x 25 x 150 cm) piece of lumber. Using a jigsaw with a 10-tooth-per-inch blade, cut all angles and the radius.

7 Rip the 2 x 10 x 60-inch (150 x 5 x 25cm) piece of cedar down to a 34 x 2 x 8¼-inch (85 x 5 x 20.6cm) piece. On one end, measure in 1½ inches (3.8cm) from the edge and mark. Draw a diagonal line from this mark to the corner point on the same edge on the opposite end of the board. Cut the line with the jigsaw.

8 On the end of the board that is 8¼ inches (20.6cm), measure in 5¾ inches (14.4cm) from the end on the straight, uncut edge and mark. Draw a diagonal line from this mark across the board to the corner to create a 34° angle. On the opposite end of the board, also on the straight, uncut edge, measure in 4½ inches (13.8cm) and mark. Draw a diagonal line from this mark across the board to the corner to create a 34° angle. This board will be the center section for the post.

9 On this center piece, measure in 7½ inches (18.8cm) from the short point side of the board and lightly mark a line the length of the board. These lines help align the board with the posts in the next step. Mark on each side of the board.

10 On the center piece, measure in 11⁷⁄₁₆ inches (28.6cm) from the short point on the 8¼-inch (20.6cm) end and mark. Measure over another 9¾ inches (24.4cm) from that mark and mark

again. Using the try square from the straightedge, draw a line across the board on these marks. Measuring from the straight edge of the board, measure over 5¾ inches (14.4cm) and draw a line between the 11⁷⁄₁₆-inch (28.6cm) and 9¾-inch (24.4cm) mark.

11 Using a jigsaw, cut out the 9¾-inch (24.4cm) area above the 5¾ inch (14.4cm) line. Using the try square, lightly draw a line across the board at the beginning of each angle on the short point side. Repeat the line on the other side of the board.

12 Place one post on a flat surface. Measure up 29½ inches (73.8cm) on the straight edge and mark. Set the center board in place with the short point side facing the straight edge of the post. The 8¼-inch (20.6cm) end of the center board should be on the bottom facing the radius cut on the post. Line up the 29½-inch (73.8cm) mark on the post with the line drawn across the center piece. Use the 1½-inch (3.1cm) line drawn the length of the outer piece to insure that there is a 1½-inch (3.1cm) overhang of the center board over the post. Attach the boards in two places using countersunk #8 1¼-inch (3cm) screws. Set the second post in place, then position and attach it in the same manner.

13 Using the two scrap pieces from the posts, rip two pieces to 2 x 5¼ x 28½ inches (5 x 13x 71.3cm). On one end of the board, measure in 2⅝ inches (6.6cm) and mark. Draw a diagonal line from this point to the corner on the opposite edge.

14 On the same edge and same end as the 2⅝-inch (6.6cm) mark, measure down 1¼ inches (3cm) and mark. Draw a diagonal line from this mark to the corner point on the same edge on the opposite end of the board.

15 On the end opposite of the marked angle, measure in 2¾ inches (6.9cm) from the end on the same edge as the long point of the angle just drawn. Measure down from the top edge 1¾ inches (4.4cm) and mark on end of board. Draw a diagonal line between the 2¾-inch (6.9cm) and 1¾-inch (4.4cm) marks. Cut all diagonals with the jigsaw. These are the arms that support the mailbox.

16 From the bottom of each post, measure up 40 inches (1m). Use a try square to mark a line across the post. Position an arm with the top of the straight, uncut edge lined up with the 40-inch (1m) mark. The wide end of the arm (5¼ inches [13.1cm]) should be on the side of the posts with the radius cut. All angles should angle back to the straight edge of the post. Position arm so there is a 5¾-inch (14.4 cm) overhang from the straight edge of the post to the long point of the arm. Attach the arm to the post with five countersunk #8 x 2-inch (5 cm) screws placed in an "X" pattern. Repeat the process on the second arm. The arms and bottom of the slot cut into the front of the center board should all be level with each other.

17 To make the mailbox cover, cut one piece of wood to ¾ x 6¾ x 9⅛ inches (1.9 x 16.9 x 22.8 cm). On the two pieces cut to ¾ x 9⅛ x 22 inches (1.9 x 22.8 x 55 cm), measure in 2¼ inches (5.6 cm) from one end of each piece and mark. On the other side of the same corner on the same end of each piece, measure over 3 inches (7.5 cm) and mark. Draw a diagonal line connecting the 2¼-inch (5.6 cm) and 3-inch (7.5 cm) marks, and cut with the jigsaw. Using the 1¼-inch (3 cm) galvanized finishing nails, nail the ¾ x 6¾ x 9⅛-inch (1.9 x 16.9 x 22.8 cm) piece at one end between the two ¾ x 9⅛ x 22-inch (1.9 x 22.8 x 55 cm) pieces. Use the nail set to countersink the nails. The ¾ x 8 x 23¾ inch (1.9 x 20 x 59.4 cm) piece will be the top of the mailbox cover, and will be nailed into place later.

18 To make the insert that will fit under the mailbox, center

the ¾ x 6 x 17¾ (1.9 x 15 x 44.4 cm) piece on the arms of the post, leaving a ¾-inch (1.9 cm) space between the back of the insert and the slot cut into the center piece of the post. (That space will be filled by the mailbox cover.) Nail the piece in place using 1¼-inch (3 cm) galvanized finishing nails. The front of the insert should be flush with the front ends of the arms.

19 Attach the mailbox cover to the post. Place the cover flush against the center notch, and attach it using countersunk #8 x 1¼-inch (3 cm) screws.

20 Insert the mailbox inside the cover and over the insert that has been nailed to the post arms. The box should fit snugly and flush with the back of the mailbox cover. Predrill three sides of the

mailbox cover ½ inch (1.3 cm) from the bottom edge. Use a ⅛-inch (3 mm) drill bit to drill through the cover and the mailbox. Use the #8 countersink bit to countersink #8 x 1¼-inch (3 cm) screws. These attach the cover and mailbox to the insert mounted on the arms.

21 Place the ¾ x 8 x 23¾ inch (1.9 x 20 x 59.4 cm) mailbox cover top piece on top of the cover and attach it using countersunk 1¼-inch (3 cm) galvanized finishing nails.

22 Working with the four ¾ x 1¾ x 22⅛ inch (1.9 x 4.4 x 55.3 cm) pieces, measure down ¾ inches (1.9 cm) from the top edge on one end of each piece and mark. On the same end, measure in ¾ inches (1.9 cm) and mark. Draw a diagonal line between the two ¾-inch (1.9 cm) marks and cut with the jigsaw. Position two of the pieces on each side of the mailbox so that the cut angle faces the front of the mailbox. The pieces should be flush with the top and ends of the mailbox. Attach each strip using countersunk 1¼-inch (3 cm) galvanized finishing nails. Measure down ¾ inch (1.9 cm) from the first strips, and attach a second strip to each side of the mailbox using the same method.

23 Attach the flag assembly from the metal mailbox to the outside of the mailbox cover, being sure to place the flag on the right side of the box as you face the box from the road. You may have to make some adjustments to ensure that the flag moves smoothly and is easily visible to the mail carrier, protruding at least 2 inches (5 cm) above the top of the mailbox cover.

24 Touch up the cedar mailbox, sanding the edges with the sand paper where necessary. Dab the bases of the ⅜-inch (9 mm) wood buttons with weatherproof wood glue and insert them into the countersunk screw holes. Allow the glue to dry completely. Apply two coats of clear oil finish according to the manufacturer's instructions, and allow the finish to dry completely before mounting the box. You may choose not to apply finish, as cedar is highly rot-resistant; without finish, the wood will weather to a grey-brown color.

RURAL FREE DELIVERY, which got its first test in 1896, meant that folks living on isolated farms no longer had to travel many miles to the closest towns for their news and other goods. Rural route letter carriers, such as this fellow delivering the mail in his horse-drawn wagon outside Milwaukee, Wisconsin, became a lifeline for inhabitants of rural areas to the outside world.

COURTESY OF THE U.S. POSTAL SERVICE.

DESIGNER
ROLF HOLMQUIST

CHAPTER
6

Woodworked Wonders

Victorian Cottage

WHETHER you're a fan of Victoriana or just love the bygone-days look of this charming miniature house, it's sure to make a lovely point of interest for your landscape.

☞ Cut List

DESC	QTY	MATERIAL	DIMENSIONS
Base plate	1	¾-inch (1.9 cm) pine	¾ x 6 x 18½ inches (1.9 x 15 x 46.3 cm)
End pieces	2	¾-inch (1.9 cm) pine	¾ x 10⅝ x 7½ inches (1.9 x 26.6 x 18.8 cm), top edges cut to 45° angle
Sides	2	⅜-inch (9 mm) tongue-and-groove wainscoting	18½ x 3½ x ½ inches (46.3 x 8.8 x 1.3 cm), cut topedge of 2 pieces to 45° angle
Roof	1	¾-inch (1.9 cm) pine	¾ x 6⅞ x 21½ inches (1.9 x 17.2 x 53.8 cm)
Roof	1	¾-inch (1.9 cm) pine	¾ x 7⅜ x 21½ inches (1.9 x 18.4 x 53.8 cm)
Dormer (flag mount)	1	standard 2 x 4 lumber	3½ x 2½ x 1½ inches (8.8 x 6.3 3.8 cm), cut on 45° angle

☞ Materials

White metal post-mount mailbox, 6½ x 8 x 19 inches (16.3 x 20 x 47.5 cm)

Lumber (see "Cut List")

1¼-inch (3 cm) galvanized deck screws

Wood glue

¾-inch (1.9 cm) brads

Victorian-style ornamental molding (see figure 2 on page 120)

Exterior white paint (or other desired color)

Shingles (leftovers from your own home, cedar, or new)

1 Wooden curtain rod end

¾-inch (1.9 cm) roofing nails

54½-inch-tall (1.4 m) Victorian-style bannister post (optional)

7 x 7 inch (17.5 x 17.5) Victorian-style shelf bracket (optional, for mounting post)

Roofing tar (optional, for post preservation)

☛ Tools

Band saw

Pencil

Drill with assorted bits

Screwdriver

Utility knife

Paintbrush

Hammer

Note: *For additional guidance in constructing the Victorian Cottage, refer to the helpful exploded-view drawing in figure 1 on page 120.*

☛ Instructions

1 Using the band saw, cut out all the wooden pieces as indicated by the "Cut List."

2 Stand the white metal mailbox upright on its front door (remove any opening latches, if necessary, to make this possible) on top of one end piece. Make sure it is centered (you should have approximately 1/2 inch [1.3 cm] remaining on either side of the arch, and 2 inches [5 cm] left above the arch) and flush with the bottom of the end piece. Trace around it with the pencil. Use the saw to cut out the traced arch. This will be the front end of the Victorian Cottage mailbox.

3 Use the saw to cut the top of each end piece to a 45° angle. Bevel one long edge on each of two pieces of wainscoting to a 45° angle. These pieces will form the tops of each side, just beneath the overhanging roof.

4 Using a drill bit slightly smaller than the 1¼-inch (3 cm) screws, drill pilot holes through the wainscoting and into the end pieces. Position the holes ¾ inch (1.9 cm) from the bottom and top of the side edge, and space them approximately 1½ inches (3.8 cm) apart. Fasten the wainscoting to the ends with the 1¼-inch (3 cm) galvanized deck screws and the screwdriver. Place the pieces with beveled edges at the top of each side.

5 To attach the roof, butt the roof pieces up against one another, with the wider piece overlapping at the roof peak. Predrill holes in the roof pieces and screw them together along the edge. Place the roof on top of the assembled mailbox structure, leaving an approximate 2-inch (5 cm) overhang at the front of the mailbox and ½-inch (1.3 cm) overhang at the back. Predrill holes through the roof into the top edge of the end pieces and the angled wainscoting side pieces. Attach the roof with the screwdriver and screws.

6 Using the wood glue and brads (for additional support), apply the ornamental molding to the front edge of the roof. Allow the glue to dry completely before handling the box.

7 Paint the Victorian mailbox white with exterior paint, or give it a coat of leftover paint in your own house color. Paint the curtain rod end the same color. Allow all pieces to dry completely. Since you are using external house paint, the mailbox should not need any extra varnish to protect it from the elements.

8 Using the utility knife, cut the shingles to fit the roof. Start at the bottom of each side of the roof and work up to the peak. Attach the shingles to the roof with the hammer and roofing nails.

9 After you have shingled the roof, attach the curtain rod end to the top of the roof. Position the curtain rod end approximately in the center of the roof, about 10 inches (25 cm) from the back edge. The curtain rod end should come with a pre-inserted screw. Simply screw the piece into the roof by hand at the desired point.

10 Mount the flag on the right side of the mailbox. To attach the flag mount, predrill two holes through the dormer piece and into the roof. Attach the dormer with screws, making sure it sits high enough on the side of the roof for the flag to extend at least 2 inches (10 cm) above the top of the box.

11 If you plan to use the Victorian post, paint the post, base plate, and brace with white exterior house paint, or exterior paint in another color of your choice.

12 To mount the mailbox on the Victorian banister post, screw the standard size white mailbox to the base plate (you may have to make new holes in the bottom of your standard mailbox to accomplish this). Predrill holes and screw the Victorian mailbox to the base plate. Attach the base plate to the top of the bannister post with screws. The base plate should be slightly off center, with a small overhang in the front. Screw the bookshelf brace to the front of the post. To help preserve the post, coat the part that will be placed in the ground with roofing tar.

Praying Mantis

NEED a life-size insect to gobble up undesirable postal parcels when no one's looking? This glorious green creature may well do the trick, preying on the latest installments of junk mail for lunch and dinner! Just make sure you teach him what's not for snacks—we'd hate for you to miss out on those zany letters from Aunt Jane in Honolulu.

☞ Materials

Lumber (see "Cut List")

3 steel plates,
¼ x 1½ x 6¾ inches
(6 mm x 3.8 cm x 16.9 cm)

Steel plate,
¼ x 1½ x 8¼ inches
(6 mm x 3.8 cm x 21 cm)

Copper-plated welding rod,
⅛ x 36 inches
(3 mm x 90 cm)

2 truck trailer clearance lights,
about 2¼-inch-diameter
(5.6 cm)

Rebar (concrete reinforcing bar),
⅜ inches x 20 feet (9 mm x 6 m)*

House paint or stain, dark green

Metal rust-proof paint, dark green

#8 x 2-inch (5 cm) galvanized screws

#8 x 3½-inch (8.75 cm) galvanized screws

#8 x 1-inch (2.5 cm) galvanized screws

1 standard metal mailbox,
with recessed bottom,
6½ x 8½ x 18¾ inches
(16.3 x 23.3 x 46.9 cm)

☞ Tools

Band saw

Small hand plane

Wood chisel

Hand saw

Wood rasp (the rougher, the better)

Sandpaper

Eye and ear protection

Mask to protect lungs

Bolt cutters, hack saw, or chop saw for cutting rebar

Vise or C-clamps

Short length of steel pipe, large enough to accommodate width of rebar

Propane torch (optional)

Protractor or magnetic angle finder (optional)

Electric drill with ⅛-, 3/16-, and ¼-inch (3, 5, and 6 mm) twist drills

Paintbrushes

Concrete mix (optional, for mounting)

Welder (or hire this job out)

☞ Cut List

DESCRIPTION	QTY	MATERIAL	DIMENSIONS
Body/Neck	1	treated landscape timber	6 inches x 6 inches x 4 feet (15 cm x 15 cm x 1.2 m)
Head	1	treated landscape timber	2 x 10 x 10 inches (5 x 25 x 25 cm)
Base plate	1	¾-inch (1.9 cm) plywood	6¼ x 17 inches (15.6 mm x 42.5 cm)

***Note:** A thicker size of rebar will form sturdier legs, but should only be used if you are able to bend it.

☛ Instructions

1 Using the photo on page 101 as a guide, sketch the side profile of the mantis body on the 4-foot (1.2 cm) length of landscape timber. Cut out the body and the sides of the neck with the band saw.

2 Using the plane, chisel or other tool, round the body to a shape similar to that of a praying mantis. You want to make two wings on the top of the back, and, on the underside of the body, seven rounded body segments that diminish slightly toward the rear. (Refer to the photograph, and think of peas in a pod for the underside of the belly. You may also wish to consult an encyclopedia or field guide drawing of a praying mantis.) Using the hand saw, cut the body segment lines about ¾ inch (1.9 cm) deep and 3½ inches (8.8 cm) apart. To form the separate body segments, chisel down into the saw cuts to remove the wood. Use the wood rasp at this point to file the segments down, then sand the body to smooth it out. Using the photos as guides, shape the head piece with the rasp and other tools. Leave two elevated circles slightly larger than the clearance lights on either side of the upper portion of the head; leave a 1-inch wide strip at surface level down the center of the face that slopes gently on either side. The bottom of the head should come to a gently rounded point (about 2 inches [5 cm] wide near the base.

3 To begin shaping the neck, use the band saw or a hand saw to cut a 45° angle at the top of the body piece. (This is where the head will attach later.) Round the sides of the neck next, leaving a flat area about 7 inches (17.5 cm) long from the bottom side of the 45° angle cut. The overall length of the body will be approximately 42½ inches (1.1 m). The neck should measure approximately 17½ inches (43.8 cm).

4 You will create three sets of appendages for the praying mantis: mailbox holder arms; front legs; and rear legs. Be sure to wear protective eye and ear gear, and wear a respirator mask to avoid inhaling metal dust. Start by cutting the 20 feet (6 m) of rebar into three sections that are approximately 75 inches (1.9 m) long (arms); 80 inches (2 m) long (front legs); and 60 inches (1.5 m) long (rear legs). Cut the rebar using a bolt cutter (place the rebar and bolt cutter on the floor, stand on the handle and use your weight to help cut the rebar); a hack saw (clamp the rebar in the vise or secure C-clamps to hold it in place while cutting); or a chop saw.

5 To fashion the mailbox holder arms, place one end of the 75-inch (1.9 m) length of rebar in the vise or C-clamps. Insert the other end into the pipe. (Using the pipe will enable you to achieve a

sharper bend in the rebar, avoiding wide curves. Also, the rebar will be easier to bend if you have a propane torch to keep it hot while you're working with it.) Using the pipe as a lever and the protracotr or angle finders to measure the angles, bend the arms into the following sequence of straight segments and angles: 7-inch (17.5 cm) segment; 75° angle bend; 13¼-inch (33 cm) segment; 45° angle; 13¼-inch (33 cm) segment; 90° angle; 3-inch (7.5 cm) segment. At this point, you have created one half of the arms. The 3-inch (7.5 cm) segment will be welded onto the mounting plate later. Working backward from the 90° angle, repeat the sequence of segments and angles to form the remaining half of the arms.

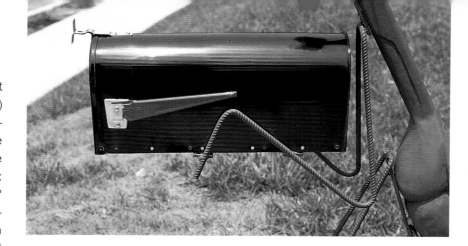

6 To fashion the front legs, insert one end of the 80-inch (2 m) length of rebar into the vise or C-clamps, and the other end into the pipe. Create the following sequence of straight segments and angles: 1½-inch (3.8 cm) segment; 45° angle; 21½ inch (53.4 cm) segment; 20° angle; 12½-inch (31.3 cm) segment; 90° horizontal angle; 3-inch (7.5 cm) segment. At this point, you have created one half of the front legs. The 3-inch (7.5 cm) segment will be welded onto the mounting plate later. Working backward from the 90° angle, repeat the sequence of segments and angles to form the remaining half of the front legs.

7 To fashion the rear legs, insert one end of the 60-inch (1.5 m) length of rebar into the vise or C-clamps, and the other end into the pipe. Create the following sequence of straight segments and angles: 1½-inch (3.8 cm) segment; 45° angle; 12-inch (30 cm) segment; 20° angle; 12½-inch (31.3 cm) segment; 90° horizontal angle; 3-inch (7.5 cm) segment. At this point, you have created one half of the rear legs. The 3-inch (7.5 cm) segment will be welded onto the mounting plate later. Working backward from the 90° angle, repeat the sequence of segments and angles to form the remaining half of the rear legs.

8 Using the bolt cutters or another tool, cut the 3-foot (90 cm) copperplated welding rod in half to form the antennae.

9 To make the mounting plate that will connect the front and rear legs to the body piece, drill one hole at each end of the ¼- x 1½- x 8¼-inch (6 mm x 3.8 cm x 20.6 cm) steel plate using the ³⁄₁₆-inch (5 mm) twist drill. Each hole should be centered (¾ inch [1.9 cm] from the outer edge of the steel plate) and placed 2 inches (5 cm) from the ends of the steel plate.

10 Repeat this process to make the two mounting plates for the mailbox and the mounting plate for the mailbox holder arms. Using the ³⁄₁₆-inch (5 mm) twist drill, drill two centered holes in each of the ¼ x 1½ x 6¾ inches (6 mm x 3.8 cm x 16.9 cm) steel plates. Position each hole 1¾ inches (4.4 cm) from one end of the plate.

11 After you have finished preparing all the pieces for assembly, paint the praying mantis body dark green with two coats of exterior house paint or wood stain. Also apply two coats of the dark green, rust-proof, metal paint to the rebar legs, antennae, and steel mounting plates. Allow the paint on all pieces to dry completely between each coat, and before assembling the structure or mounting the mailbox.

12 To attach the rebar legs to the steel mounting plates, lay the praying mantis body on the floor in the desired position. Then, lightly weld the leg segments in place on the mounting plates; you can bend them back and forth to separate them from the mounting plate and reposition them, if necessary. Getting the legs in just the right place may be a trial and error process—just remember that every bug is different! As long as your bug will stand up, you're doing fine! Once you've got the legs where you want them, weld them securely to the mounting plates.

13 After you have welded the front and rear legs onto the ¼- x 1½- x 8¼-inch (6 mm x 3.8 cm x 20.6 cm) steel mounting plate, attach the plate to the body. Position the plate so that the top hole rests near the top of the second body segment; the bottom hole will sit at the top of the third body segment. Mark the locations of the two holes on the body piece, then predrill holes in the body and attach the mounting plate with two #8 x 2-inch (5 cm) galvanized screws.

14 To mount the mailbox, insert the base plate in the recessed bottom of the mailbox. Secure the base plate with #8 x 2-inch (5 cm) galvanized screws, inserting three screws (placed near the front, middle, and back of the box) through pre-existing holes on each side of the mailbox (if your mailbox has no holes, drill three hles through the side edges of the recessed bottom). Once the base plate is securely attached, set the mailbox on the arms. With a pencil, mark the location of the four holes in the steel mounting plates on the bottom of the base plate. Pre-drill holes in the base plate at the marked locations. Place the mailbox on the arms again and attach it with two #8 x 1-inch (2.5 cm) galvanized screws inserted up through the steel plate into the bottom of the base plate.

15 Mount the eyes on the praying mantis head by popping the lens off the clearance lights and inserting a screw through the middle of each light into the head. Position the eyes in the wider upper region of the head.

16 In the top edge of the head, drill two ⅛-inch (3 mm) holes about 2 inches (5 cm) apart. Insert the two antennae into the holes after you have mounted the head on the body.

17 To mount the head on the praying mantis, place the head piece on the angled end of the neck and insert two #8 x 3½-inch (8.8 cm) galvanized screws through the back of the neck into the head piece.

18 Finally, stand your praying mantis up and marvel at your creation. To mount the praying mantis mailbox in your yard or at the curbside, you have two options: either make a small wooden mold, pour a concrete slab, and place the front legs into the concrete as it hardens; or, weld two leftover rebar stubs to the ends of the rear legs, at a 90° angle, and insert the stubs firmly into the ground. Both of these options should hold the mailbox firmly in place.

Mail Note...

Behind the Scenes

Ever watched your local mail carrier stagger under the load of his or her mailbag and wondered, "How do they do it?" Multiply by a staggering sum the number of letters and the like a single carrier has in his or her charge on any given day, and you begin to get a picture of the daunting task the U.S. Postal Service has on its hands six days a week. (It's enough to make you forgive that occasional late or lost piece of correspondence!) The U.S. Postal Service:

- **SERVICES** 312,000 collection boxes and 38,019 post offices, hitting some 130 million delivery points each year

- **INCLUDES** 331 processing plants where mail is sorted and shipped, using some 75,184 pieces of mail-processing equipment to cope with—among other things—38 million changes of address per year

- **MAINTAINS** 192,904 vehicles covering 1.1 billion miles annually to pick up, transport, and deliver the mail, with 2.7 billion pounds of mail carried on commercial airline flights

- **SERVES** 7 million customers transacting business in post offices daily, while 234,033 mail carriers deliver some 3.4 billion pieces of mail every week across the country

- **HANDLES** 630 million pieces of mail each day—41 percent of the world's mail volume (Japan comes in second, handling 6 percent)

- **EMPLOYS** a career staff of more than 750,000, making it the country's largest civilian employer

Antique Truck

DESIGNER
**ROLF
HOLMQUIST**

A MUST for classic car aficionados, this attractive mailbox is bound to rev up anyone's day. It's a great project for folks with moderate woodworking skills, and the finished box adds a dash of fun to any roadside spot.

☞ Materials

Fender pattern (see figure 2 on page 118)

Lumber (see "Cut List")

Black metal post-mount mailbox, 6½ x 8¾ x 19 inches (16.3 x 21.9 x 47.5 cm)

Exterior enamel or latex paint in black, grey, red, silver, or other desired colors

Clear acrylic spray varnish (optional)

Self-adhesive mylar numbers for house number

Plastic lid, 4⅝-inch-diameter (11.6 cm) (optional)

Black spray paint (optional)

Black permanent marker (optional)

1 ½-inch (3.8 cm) galvanized screws

Nails 1-inch (2.5 cm)

4 washers, 1½ inches (3.8 cm)

4 hexagonal bolts, 2-inch (5 cm) diameter

2 rimmed lids from metal cans, approx. 3-inch (7.5 cm) diameter (for headlights)

Self-adhesive vinyl alphabet stickers (optional, to post your name)

2 brads or upholstery tacks

☞ Tools

Carbon paper

Pencil

Saber or band saw

Paintbrushes (small and large)

Tape measure

Drill

¾-inch (1.9 cm) and 1¾-inch (4.4 cm) drill bits

Hammer

☛ Instructions

1 Enlarge by photocopying the fender pattern in figure 2 on page 118. Use carbon paper to trace four fenders onto the fender pieces. Then, using the saber or band saw, cut out all the wooden pieces as indicated in the "Cut List."

2 Stand the mailbox upright on its front door (remove any opening latches, if necessary, to make this possible) on top of one end piece and trace around it with the pencil. Use the saw to cut out the traced arch. This will be the front end of your truck mailbox.

3 Paint both end pieces gray. On the front end (the piece with the arch cut out), draw the windshield, making a 7- x 4½-inch (17.5 x 11.3 cm) rectangle starting ½ inch (1.3 cm) below the top of the piece. On the back end piece, draw the rear window, a 3- x 5⅜-inch (7.5 x 13.4 cm) oval placed 1½ inches (3.8 cm) below the top edge and centered 1¼ inches (3 cm) in from each side edge. Paint the windshield and rear window black.

4 Paint the roof black, applying at least two coats for good coverage. Also paint the base plate, bottom pieces, and fenders black. Paint the two dowel pieces (for taillights) red.

5 Paint the edge of the mailbox door silver to create the radiator. Also paint the upper tab of the mailbox latch silver to simulate a hood ornament. Outline the indented rectangle on the mailbox door (or draw a 4½- x 2¼-inch [11.3 x 5.6 cm] rectangle on the box door) in silver and apply the self-adhesive numbers of your address to form the license plate.

6 To paint the wheels, find a lid or circular shape that will leave a ¾-inch (1.9 cm) border around the edge of the wheel when placed in the center of the wooden circle. Either trace around the shape and paint the border black by hand, or secure the shape to the wheel and spray paint the wheel black. Paint black

☛ Cut List

DESCRIPTION	QTY	MATERIAL	DIMENSIONS
Base plate	1	¾-inch (1.9 cm) pine	6 x 18½ inches (15 x 46.3 cm)
Bottom pieces	2	¾-inch (1.9 cm) pine	3¼ x 22 inches (8 x 55 cm)
Center bottom piece	1	¾-inch (1.9 cm) pine	2 x 6 inches (5 x 15 cm)
End pieces	2	¾-inch (1.9 cm) pine	7½ x 13¾ inches (18.8 x 34.4 cm)
Roof pieces	1	¾-inch (1.9 cm) pine	11¼ x 17 inches (28 x 42.5 cm)
Wheel pieces	4	¾-inch (1.9 cm) pine	6¼ inches (15.6 cm) diameter x ¾ inches
Fender pieces	4	¾-inch (1.9 cm) pine	3½ x 10 inches (8.8 x 25 cm)
Side pieces	12 (6 each side)	Tongue-and-groove scrap oak flooring or wainscoting	13¾ x 14 inches (34.4 x 35 cm)
Braces	2	¾-inch (1.9 cm) pine	1¾ inches wide at top x 13¾ inches (34.4 cm) tall
Taillight pieces	2	½-inch (1.3 cm) wooden dowel	½ inch (1.3 cm) long

Note: For additional guidance in making the Antique Truck, refer to the helpful exploded-view drawing on page 118.

tires on both sides of each wheel, and paint the rims of all wheels. Draw eight ¾-inch-wide (1.9 cm) spokes on the outside of each wheel. Paint the inside of each spoke silver. Let the spokes dry completely, then outline each spoke with black paint or permanent marker.

7 Predrill holes and attach the base plate to the bottom pieces with the 1½-inch (3.8 cm) galvanized screws. Place three screws along the base plate on each side, approximately 8 inches (20 cm) apart. Use two screws, 4¾ inches (11.9 cm) apart, to secure the base plate to the center bottom piece.

8 Use the 1½-inch (3.8 cm) galvanized screws to fasten the side pieces to the end pieces. Predrill holes and insert one screw into each end of each piece of tongue and groove flooring, stacking six on each side of the truck. Paint the ends of the side pieces to match the end pieces.

9 Position the roof on the truck so that there is a 2-inch (5 cm) overhang in the front and a ½-inch (1.3 cm) overhang in the back. Predrill holes and screw the roof onto the truck by placing one screw into the top of a side piece at each corner.

10 Attach the braces to the front edge of the side pieces. Hammer three evenly spaced nails into the front of each brace. The braces will help support the roof overhang in the front of the truck.

11 Position and mark the location of the wheels on the outer edge of the bottom pieces. Predrill holes in the bottom pieces and the wheels, then attach the wheels using the washers and bolts.

12 Predrill holes and screw the fenders onto the truck base, using two screws in the flat part of each fender. Note that the flat part of the fender faces the back of the truck on the front fenders, and faces the front of the truck on the back fenders.

13 Attach the can lids to the top of the front fenders to form the headlights. Position each can lid about halfway down the arch on the front of the fender. Predrill a hole in the fender and the lid, and screw into place.

14 Facing the truck from the front, attach the flag to the right side of the truck's roof. You may have to perform some cosmetic surgery on the flag that came with your mailbox to get it ready for roof-mounting. Secure the flag base to the roof with two screws.

15 Apply the self-adhesive vinyl letters to the flag-side of the mailbox. A good way to make sure the stickers will appear balanced and even is to lay the letters out on your work surface and find the middle letter of your name. Start applying the letters to the side of the truck with this letter, or two letters, and work outward to the first and last letters of your name.

16 Position each taillight ½ inch (1.3 cm) in from the outer edge of the bottom pieces at the back of the truck. Predrill hole and attach the taillights by nailing one brad into each piece. Upholstery tacks will also work well.

17 Attach the mailbox to your post and install it in the location you've chosen.

A Gallery of Mailboxes

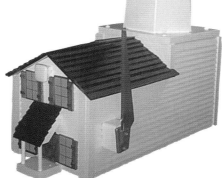

TOP LEFT: Bob Brown's Custom Hog, The Mailbox Factory

TOP RIGHT: Stony Point Lighthouse, The Mailbox Installers

CENTER: Great White Shark, The Mailbox Installers

LEFT AND ABOVE: Mr. Gusette's Pride and Joy, mailbox and original. The Mailbox Factory

GALLERY
G
The Ultimate Mailbox Book

GALLERY

G

The Ultimate
Mailbox Book

ABOVE: Country Cottage,
The Mailbox Factory

TOP RIGHT AND BOTTOM LEFT:
Covered Bridge, Bavarian
Chalet, The Mailbox
Installers

FAR RIGHT: Loaf of Bread, The
Mailbox Factory

Note: For company contact information,
see "Acknowledgments," page 126.

A Gallery of Mailboxes

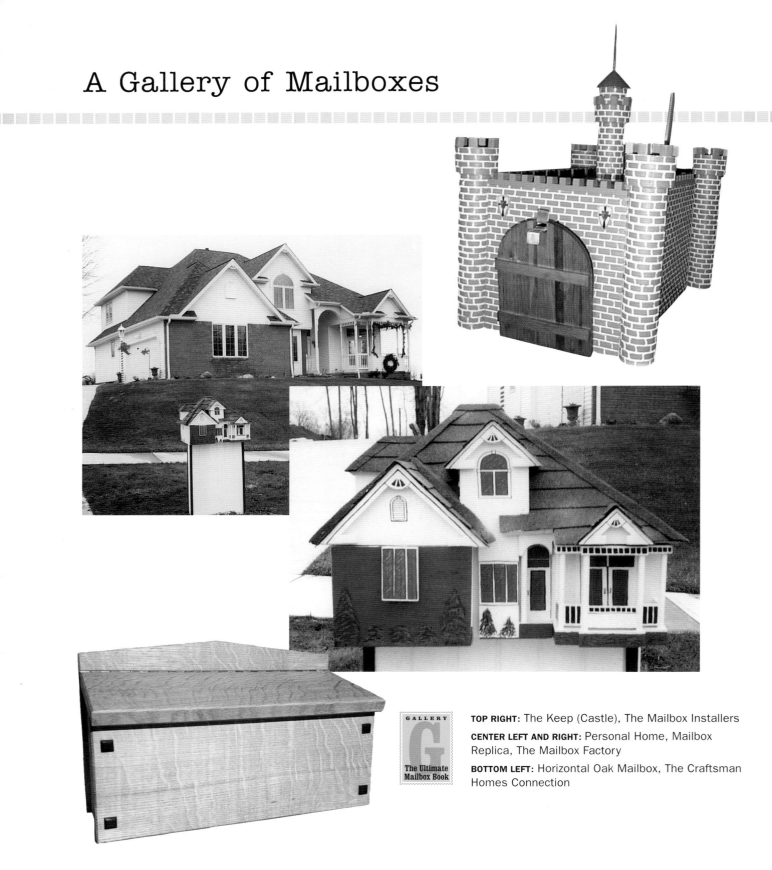

TOP RIGHT: The Keep (Castle), The Mailbox Installers

CENTER LEFT AND RIGHT: Personal Home, Mailbox Replica, The Mailbox Factory

BOTTOM LEFT: Horizontal Oak Mailbox, The Craftsman Homes Connection

GALLERY

G

The Ultimate
Mailbox Book

TOP LEFT: Custom Horse Mailbox, The Mailbox Installers

CENTER: U.S. Junk Mail, Woodendipity

BOTTOM LEFT AND RIGHT: Smooth Copper Mailbox, Saddlebag Mailbox, The Craftsman Homes Connection

Noah's Ark
Page 83

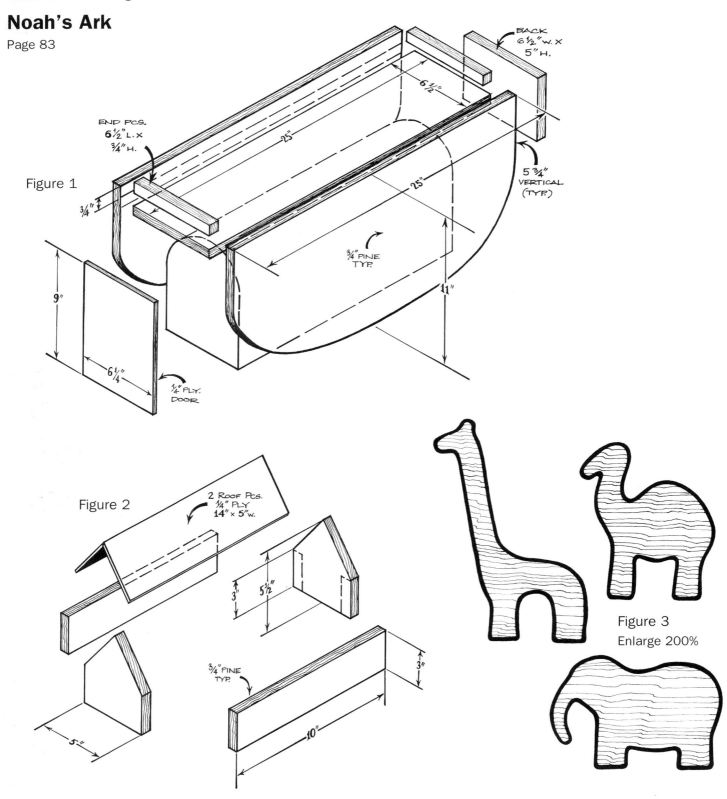

Figure 1

END PCS.
6½" L. x
¾" H.

¾"

9"

6¼"

¼" PLY.
DOOR

25"

6½"

25"

¾" PINE
TYP.

11"

5¾"
VERTICAL
(TYP.)

BACK
6½" W. x
5" H.

Figure 2

2 ROOF PCS.
¼" PLY
14" x 5" W.

3"

5½"

5"

¾" PINE
TYP.

10"

3"

Figure 3
Enlarge 200%

Jungle Fun Decoupage

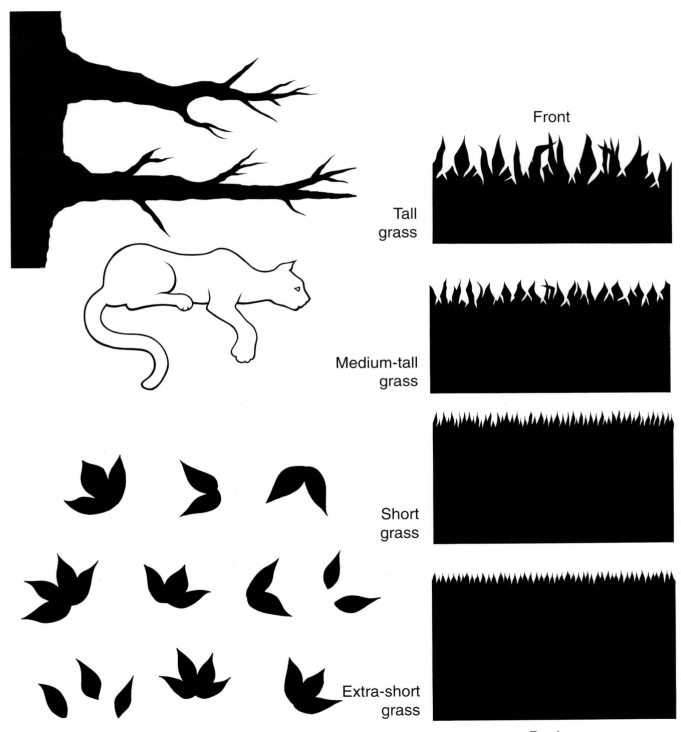

Front

Tall grass

Medium-tall grass

Short grass

Extra-short grass

Back

Covered Bridge

Page 78

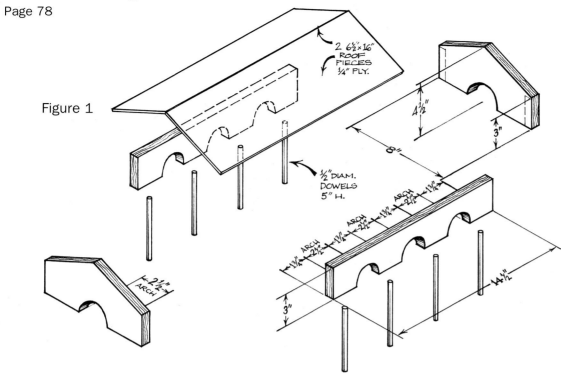

Figure 1

2 6½" x 16"
ROOF
PIECES
¼" PLY.

4½"

3"

8"

½" DIAM.
DOWELS
5" H.

ARCH 1¾"
2½" 1¾"
ARCH
2½" 1¾"
ARCH
2½" 1¾"
1¾"

3"

14½"

2½"
ARCH

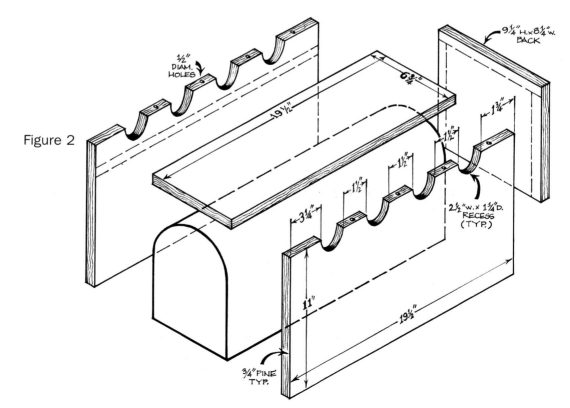

Figure 2

½"
DIAM.
HOLES

9¼" H. x 8¼" W.
BACK

6¾"

19½"

1¾"

1½"

1½"

1½"

1½"

1½"

3¼"

2½" w. x 1¼" D.
RECESS
(TYP.)

11"

19½"

¾" PINE
TYP.

Woodburned Van Gogh

Page 59

Figure 1

Rustic Birch

Page 31

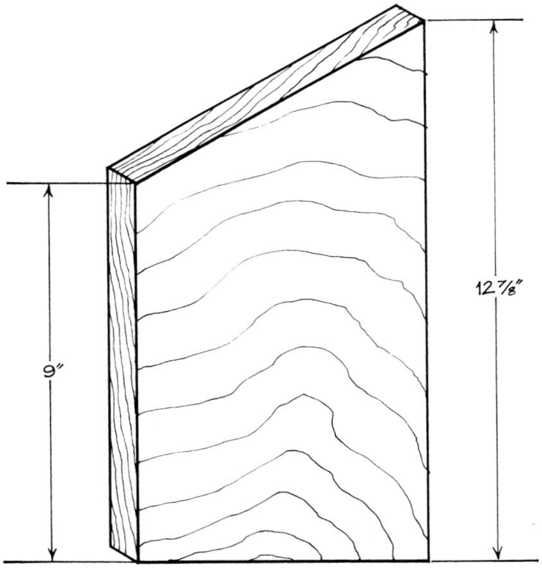

12⅞"

9"

9¾"

Figure 3 Sides

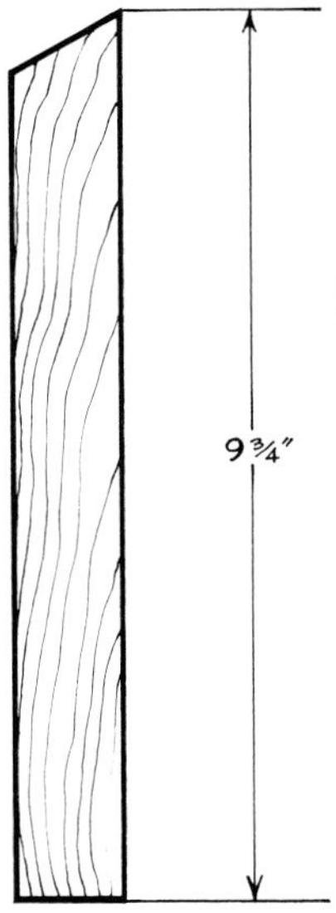

Figure 4 Front

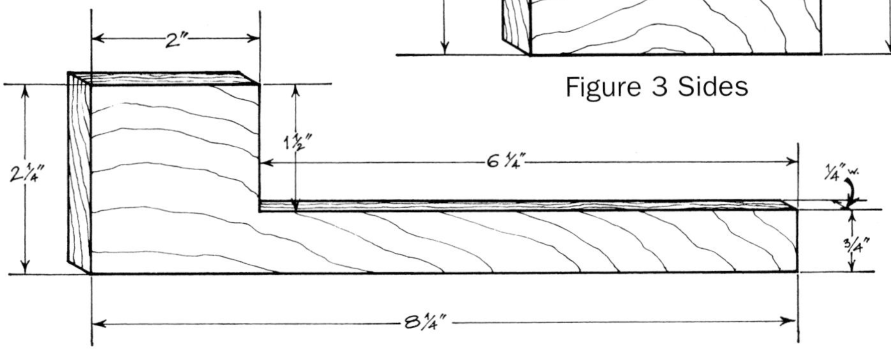

2"

1½"

6¼"

¼" w.

2¼"

¾"

Figure 2 Flag

8¼"

Antique Truck

Page 106

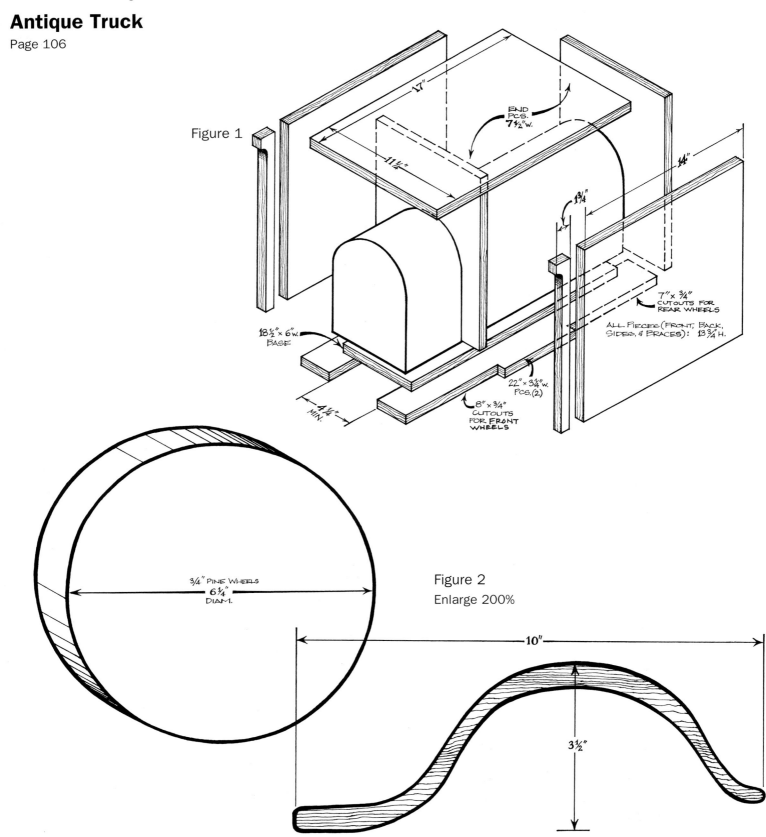

Figure 1

17"

END PCS. 7½" W.

11¼"

14"

1¾"

18½" × 6" W. BASE

7" × ¾" CUTOUTS FOR REAR WHEELS

ALL PIECES (FRONT, BACK, SIDES, & BRACES): 13¾ H.

4¼" MIN.

22" × 3¾" W. PCS. (2)

8" × ¾" CUTOUTS FOR FRONT WHEELS

¾" PINE WHEELS
6¼" DIAM.

Figure 2
Enlarge 200%

10"

3½"

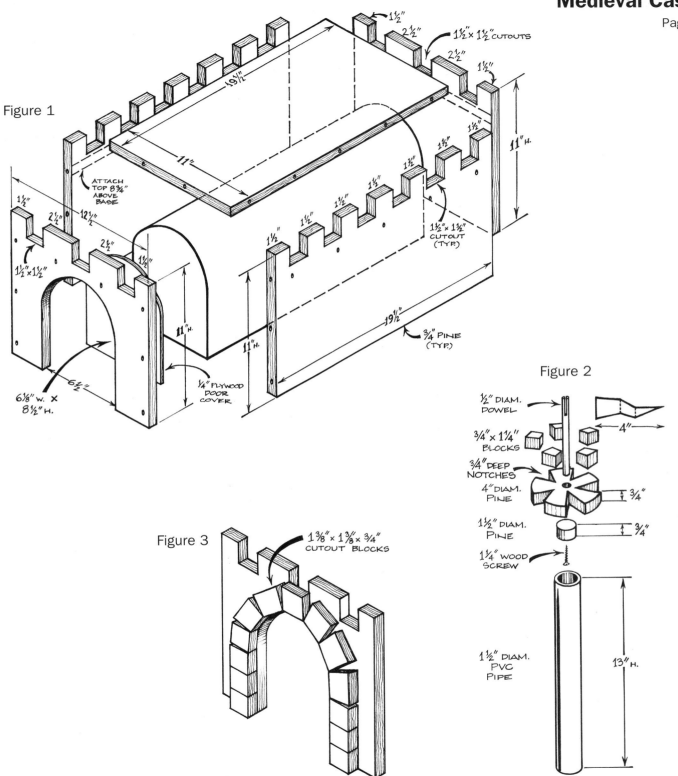

Figure 1

1½"
2½"
1½" × 1½" CUTOUTS
2½"
1½"
11" H.
19½"
11"
ATTACH TOP 8¾" ABOVE BASE
1½"
2½"
12½"
2½"
1½"
1½" × 1½"
1½"
1½"
1½"
1½"
1½"
1½"
1½"
1½"
1½"
1½" × 1½" CUTOUT (TYP.)
11" H.
11" H.
19½"
¾" PINE (TYP.)
¼" PLYWOOD DOOR COVER
6⅛" W. × 8½" H.
6½"

Figure 2

½" DIAM. DOWEL
¾" × 1¼" BLOCKS
¾" DEEP NOTCHES
4" DIAM. PINE
1½" DIAM. PINE
1¼" WOOD SCREW
1½" DIAM. PVC PIPE
4"
¾"
¾"
13" H.

Figure 3

1⅜" × 1⅜" × ¾" CUTOUT BLOCKS

Victorian Cottage

Page 98

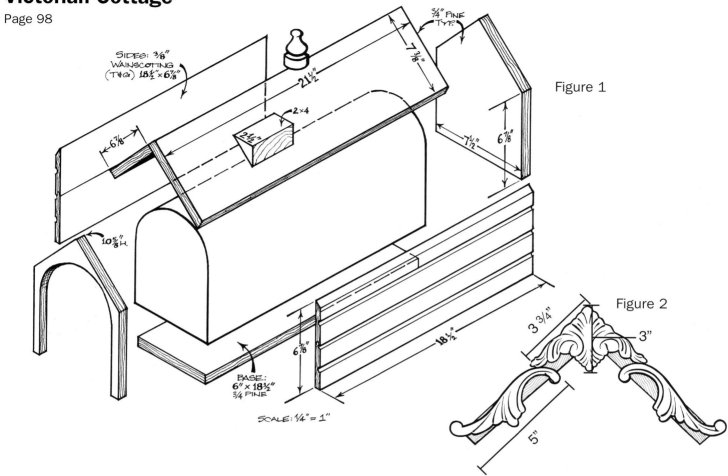

SIDES: 3/8"
WAINSCOTING
(T&G) 18½" × 6⅞"

3/4" PINE TYP.

21½"

7 3/8"

2×4

2½"

6⅞"

7½"

6⅞"

Figure 1

10⅝" H.

BASE:
6" × 18½"
3/4 PINE

6⅞"

18½"

SCALE: ¼" = 1"

Figure 2

3 3/4"

3"

5"

Little Country House

Page 40

Figure 3

Enlarge 200%

Taj Mahal
Page 63

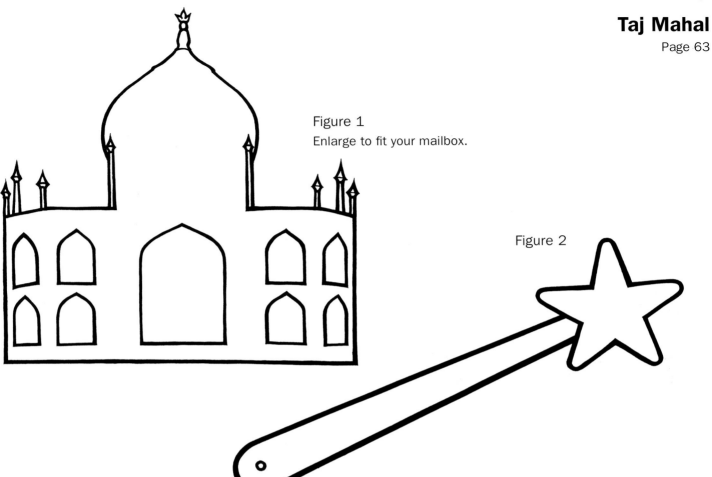

Figure 1
Enlarge to fit your mailbox.

Figure 2

Spring Garden
Page 28

Figure 3

Enlarge to various
sizes as desired.

Dutch Flowerpots

Page 73

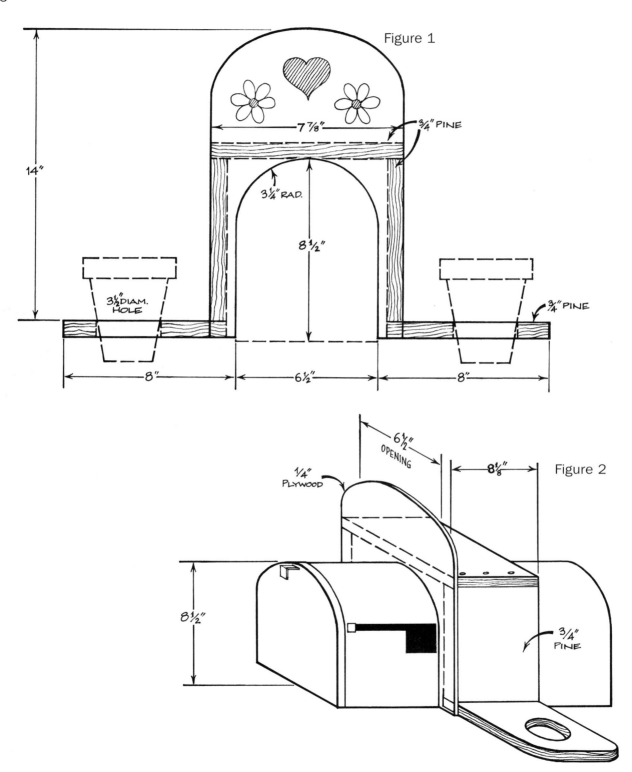

Figure 1

14"

7 7/8"

3/4" PINE

3 1/4" RAD.

8 1/2"

3 1/2" DIAM. HOLE

3/4" PINE

8"   6 1/2"   8"

6 1/2" OPENING

8 1/8"

Figure 2

1/4" PLYWOOD

8 1/2"

3/4" PINE

Pink & White Dogwood

Figure 1
Enlarge 200%

Figure 2
Enlarge 200%

Contributing Designers

ROBIN and **HELEN CLARK** own Robin's Wood Ltd., in Asheville, North Carolina, where they manufacture outdoor products for people and wildlife. Robin's Wood, 2000 Riverside Drive, Asheville, NC, 28804. Website: www.robinswood.com. Email: robin@robinswood.com.

MAUREEN (Cha Cha) DONAHUE is a graphic artist who also makes and sells furniture and wooden and ceramic clocks. Much as she loves her three cats, she still misses her Harley. She lives in Asheville, North Carolina.

KATHERINE DUNCAN currently spends her days working as an editor and author for Lark Books in Asheville, North Carolina, and somehow finds time to create fabulous projects on the side. Prior to her present occupation, Katherine worked for many years as a museum curator and director. She has had a lifelong interest in writing and the arts.

MIKE DURKIN teaches middle school technology in Laurinburg, South Carolina, where he lives with his wife, Carol; son, Scott; and dog, Roscoe. When it comes to crafting, he and Carol make an expert team: He does the drafting and building, she applies paint and finishing touches.

NORRIS HALL is a professional artist in Murfreesboro, Tennessee, whose talents range from wood sculpture to illustration. In addition to eating, sleeping, and working, he shares a home with his wife, two daughters, two dogs, and one cat. Norris Hall Studios, 341 County Farm Rd., Murfreesboro, TN, 37127.

MARGARET (Peggy) HAYES creates custom painted furniture and cross-stitch designs. She credits much of her inspiration to her husband of 28 years, Charles, with whom she shares a home in Fletcher, North Carolina.

Swedish-born artist **ROLF HOLMQUIST** lives and creates in the mountains of western North Carolina, where he and his wife, Diane, are building a log cabin to share with their dog, Daisy May, and two new kittens, Patches and Peaches. Rolf's art revolves around drawing and the incorporation of "found" items; his collection includes an award-winning array of medical embossings. Sunrise Studios, 900 Sparmill Hollow, Burnsville, NC, 28714 (828) 675-5077.

Whether painting houses or canvases, **GARY ISRINGHAUS**, commonly known as Isha, has been an artist all his life. He began his academic studies at the Art Center College of Design in Los Angeles, California, and went on to get his B.F.A. From Sonoma State University, followed by a master's degree from the University of Southern California. When he's not painting, he enjoys observing the exploits of his two cats, Eva and Simba, at his Weaverville, North Carolina, home.

LAUREY-FAYE LONG is an all-around crafter from Marshall, North Carolina, where she lives with her husband, woodworker Steve Tengelsen, and a host of four-legged creatures, ranging from cat and hound-dog to the goat and sheep they recently acquired to help mow the grass.

SHELLEY LOWELL is a painter, sculptor, illustrator, graphic designer, and frequent contributor of projects for Lark Books. She received her BFA at Pratt Institute in New York, and now teaches a variety of art classes. She lives and works in Arlington, Virginia.

TAMARA MILLER is a mom first and crafter second who lives in Hendersonville, North Carolina, with her husband, Jeff, and son, Beck. She is especially motivated by projects that allow her to incorporate the interests of her family while utilizing her creativity.

JEAN TOMASO MOORE "dabbles" in a wide range of art media and can craft anything she sets her mind to. Designing mailboxes held special appeal for Jean—not only has her brother, Jack, delivered mail in New Jersey for 20 years, but both she and her husband, Richard, are former mail carriers who continue to work for the postal service in Asheville, North Carolina.

RHEA ORMOND lives and works as a professional artist in the small, quiet town of Burnsville, North Carolina, with her son, Jeffrey. Her specialties include painting murals around the country and teaching college art and humanities. She can be reached at the Academy Street School of the Arts, Burnsville, NC 28714, or by e-mail at rheaormond@mailexcite.com.

Artist **BETH PALMER** decorated the mailbox that hangs outside her home in Greensboro, North Carolina, before she even knew we were doing this book! When she's not painting mailboxes, she explores many other avenues of the art world, creating everything from murals and decorative arts to home accessories. In addition to creating her own artwork, Beth teaches art to children of all ages.

Now living "the good life" on four and a half acres of quiet land outside of Lincoln, Illinois, retired carpenter **DON SHULL** spends summers in his flower garden and winters in his work shop. These seasonal crafts complement each other well: summers allow him to observe the garden bugs he describes as "fascinating," while colder weather affords him time to recreate them in everything from whirligigs to, as of this book, mailboxes!

M.C. (Cathy) SMITH is an artist who works in a variety of media. She is currently following her destiny in western North Carolina, accompanied and encouraged in this pursuit by her husband, son, and assorted feline, canine, and reptilian family members.

MELISSA ANNE STOWERS has painted all her life. She now enjoys creating freelance artwork in the shadow of the Smoky Mountains in Granger County, Tennessee, where she lives on a small farm with her husband, Johnny, three dogs, five horses, and one adopted burro. PO Box 253, Blaine, TN, 37709.

MARK STROM lives in Asheville, North Carolina, with his wife and three children. His studio, where he produces elegantly simple and straightforward wood sculpture inspired by the tree-covered mountains and his Scandinavian heritage, stands beside the Swannanoa River. It is from his family and his surroundings that his work draws its beauty and inspiration. Lothlorien Woodworking, 244 B. Swannanoa River Road, Asheville, NC 28805.

ELLEN ZAHOREC is a mixed-media studio artist in Cincinnatti, Ohio, who specializes in hand-made paper and collage. Her work, shown internationally, is part of numerous private and corporate collections.

Acknowledgments

Many, many thanks to the following people, businesses, and organizations who so generously and graciously helped make this book happen.

For their enthusiasms about the book and kind donations of mailboxes for use by designers:

Barb Seefeld
Mahvelous Mailboxes
N888 W16691 Appleton Ave.
Menomonee Falls, WI 53051-2852
PHONE: 888-675-6245
WEBSITE: www.mahvelousmailboxes.com

Salsbury Industries Mailboxes
1010 E. 62nd St.
Los Angeles, CA, 90001-1598
PHONE: 800-SALSBURY
WEBSITE: www.salsbury.com

For providing fantastic historical photographs: Daniel Afzal at the United States Postal Service Photo Department in Washington, D.C., and all the other wonderful folks listed below:

Paul Reynolds
California Mailboxes
844 N. Main St.
Orange, CA 92868
PHONE: 714-771-0248
FAX: 714-771-0252
EMAIL: Calmailbox@ APC.net
WEBSITE: www.mailboxes.residential.com

Bruce Duculon and Julie Hunkar
The Mailbox Installers
350 Center St., #78
Miamiville, OH 45147
PHONE: 513-831-1987
FAX: 513-576-6513
WEBSITE: www.mailboxinstallers.com

Wayne Burwell
The Mailbox Factory
7857 Chardon Rd.
Kirtland, OH 44094-9579
PHONE: 440-256-MAIL or 888-740-MAIL
FAX: 440-256-6728
WEBSITE: www.mailboxfactory.com

John Robison
The Craftsman Homes Connection
PMB 343
2525 E. 29th, Suite 10B
Spokane, WA 99223
PHONE: 509-535-5098
FAX: 509-534-8916
EMAIL: elvis@crafthome.com
WEBSITE: www.crafthome.com

Robert DuLong
Woodendipity, Inc.
9485 River St.
Phoenix, NY 13135-1501
PHONE: 800-876-1928
FAX: 315-695-2006
EMAIL: rdulong@woodendipity.com
WEBSITE: www.woodendipity.com

For his kind contribution of metal-working services and advice:

Stefan Bonitz
Steebo Design
86 S. Lexington Ave., #4
Asheville, NC 28801
828-253-4610

For opening their wonderful yards and gardens to us for photography purposes:

John Cram
Peter Loewer
Dr. Peter and Jasmine Gentling
Kay Stafford
Colleen Sikes
Patrick and Laura Doran
Craig Weis and Kathy Holmes
Terry Taylor and Jeff Webb
Todd and Catherine Kaderabek
Jane and Jim LaFerla
Molly Bryant

For sharing their tales of various treats and tribulations of the mail carrier's life (Fair weather and friendly dogs to you!):

Kathie Grable
Tony Hribar
Joyce Whipple

For his keen eye, sense of humor, and patience, Chris Bryant, art director; for his super photography and congeniality, Evan Bracken; for his all-around styling and organizational help, Skip Wade; for his hard work as always, Hannes Charen, production assistant.

Index